D0917899

R H West

Old Ashmolean Reprints

II

ELIAS ASHMOLE
Aged 73, 1689

THE DIARY AND WILL OF ELIAS ASHMOLE, EDITED AND EXTENDED FROM THE ORIGINAL MANUSCRIPTS BY R. T. GUNTHER

OXFORD

1927

From all booksellers, price 7s. 6d. net.

Made and Printed in Great Britain by
Butler & Tanner Ltd., Frome and London

PREFACE

THE biographers of Ashmole seldom omit to recall the concluding words of the epitaph on his monument in Lambeth —*Durante Musaeo Ashmoleano Oxonii nunquam moriturus*—" while the Ashmolean Museum endures, he will never die."

It is unfortunate that nowadays an ambiguity has been introduced where there should have been none. The application of the term "Ashmolean" to miscellaneous collections brought together in a modern structure that has grown out of a building previously, and more correctly known by the names of other benefactors, as the Randolph Gallery and the Taylor Building, or more concisely as the University Galleries. Ashmole's name should stand, not for art and archæology, or for more or less important bric-à-brac, but for his incomparably greater achievement, the establishment of the first Museum of Natural History in Britain.

For close on two hundred years the

original Ashmolean Museum, including as it did the collections of the Tradescants, was one of the treasuries of Oxford, a unique heritage, ranking with the Bodleian and the Physick Garden. Natural Science and the History of Science could there be studied side by side in an Institution founded for the purpose. In the scientific onrush of the last century these historic collections were dispersed, and during the first quarter of our own century the building, the finest and most venerable museum building in Britain, remained derelict.

The reopening in the present day of a portion of the " old " Ashmolean as a Science Museum, has seemed a fitting occasion for a revision of the " Diary " of the Founder, of which Ashmole bequeathed the original to be kept with other of his manuscripts in the Museum. It was printed twice in 1717, and again in 1774. Like the other rarities, it has not been suffered to remain where he had intended.

The *Diary* shows how step by step the son of a Lichfield saddler worked his way into Society. He was in modern parlance a " climber," making use of early friends, marrying judiciously, practising alchemy, astrology, fortune-telling, healing and heraldry to accomplish his ends. A born collector too, collecting influential acquaintance much as he collected gold chains, medals, and books : doubtless for the gratification that a vain man would feel in being widely known as " the greatest virtuoso and curioso " of his time, but with a deeper purpose also.

Not that we think Ashmole to have been aware of the great work he was doing. He would probably have cited his *History of the Order and Institution of the Garter* as the great work of his life. The sequel has shown the History of the Garter to have been the means by which the crowning achievement became possible. The European reputation the author thereby acquired gave him a standing in the great world, which made easy the acceptance of his rarities by the authorities of the University, even though a large sum had to be found to preserve and instal in a worthy building the Natural History Collections of the Tradescants.

It is for the founding of the first public *Museum of Natural History* in Britain that Ashmole will be honoured, for this that his name will be remembered not only as long as his Museum lasts, as John Aubrey thought, but wherever Museums of Natural History are recognized as important factors in education. Do we not owe the most notable theory of our day, the theory of evolution, to the orderly and systematic arrangement of animals and plants in Museums of Natural History ?

In reopening the Old Ashmolean Building for Scientific Instruments the University has made a step in the right direction of a worthy memorial to Ashmole, which, strange to say, has so long been wanting in Oxford. An armorial window has been erected to his honour by the generosity of Brasenose College. Professor Goodrich has kindly permitted a few relics from the oldest London Museum, the Science Museum of the Tradescants, to be shown in the historic building which Ashmole caused to be built for them in 1683.

The good work should be continued, and there should be restored to Oxford what was lost when most of the original contents of the oldest of all Science Museums in Britain were scattered or burnt, and the residue divided amongst the new University Museum, the Galleries of Art and Archæology, the Botanic Garden and the Bodleian Library.

A unique old-world treasure house was then dismantled, with no compensating gain to learning.

R. T. GUNTHER.

Magdalen College, Oxford.

26 *November*, 1926.

** While these pages are passing through the press, our friends in Virginia, recognizing the international importance of the work of these pioneers, have presented an armorial window to the memory of Ashmole's friend, John Tradescant the younger, to commemorate his two visits to Virginia in 1642 and 1654, and so to add yet another link between the New and the Old Worlds.

The window was unveiled on behalf of the donors by Lord Fairfax of Cameron, and it was received on behalf of the University by the Vice-Chancellor, the Warden of All Souls College.

It is hoped that other windows, to Ashmole's friends Dr. Robert Plot, the first Keeper of his Museum, and to Sir Christopher Wren, may be added in 1927.

PREFACE TO THE EDITION
OF 1717

THE bare Mention of the Person, whose Diary and Letters are now published, may sufficiently satisfie the World from whence they originally came, and where they are still preserved : The Copy, from whence these Papers are published, is in the Hand-Writing of ROBERT PLOT, *L. D. late Professor of Chymistry, Chief Keeper of the* Ashmolean Musæum *in the University of* Oxford, *and Secretary of the Royal Society, and was by him transcribed for the Use of a near Relation of Mr.* Ashmole's, *a private Gentleman in* Staffordshire, *who has been pleased to think they may be acceptable to the World for their Exactness and Singularity.* They were collated a few Years since by David Parry, *M. A. of* Jesus *College in* Oxford, *and Head-Keeper of the same Place, who corrected from the original Manuscript* [1] *some few literal Errors.* The Character of Mr. Ashmole *is so well known, and so excellently, though concisely drawn in*

[1] MS. *Ashmole* 1136.

thefe Papers, *as well as in that Article publifhed under his Name, in the* Supplement *to the learned Mr.* Collier's *Hiftorical Dictionary, partly extracted from thefe Materials by the juftly celebrated Mr.* Edward Llwyd, *Superior Bedel of Divinity in the Vniverfity of* Oxford, *that no Recommendation of an obfcure Editor can be of any Service, after fo noted Names : The Vfefulnefs of this Kind of Works I fhall not defcant upon ; but only fay thus much, That they let us into the fecret Hiftory of the Affairs of their feveral Times : Difcover the Springs of Motion, and difplay many valuable, though minute Circumftances overlooked, or unknown to our general Hiftorians, and to conclude all, fatiate our largeft Curiofity.*

Newington,
Feb. 1716–17.

CHARLES BURMAN.

THE LIFE OF
ELIAS ASHMOLE, ESQ. ;
IN THE WAY OF DIARY.

Written by Himself.

I ELIAS ASHMOLE, was the son and only child of Simon Ashmole of Lich-field, sadler, eldest son to Mr. Thomas Ash-mole of the said city, sadler, twice chief Bayliff of that Corporation, and of Anne, one of the daughters of Anthony Bowyer of the city of Coventry, draper, and Bridget his wife, only daughter to Mr. —— Fitch of Ausley in the County of Warwick, Gent.

I was born the 23rd of May 1617 (and as my dear and good mother hath often told me) near half an hour after 3 o'clock in the morning.[1]

[1] The site of A's birthplace, a house in Breadmarket Street, now occupied as offices by Messrs. Winterton & Sons, was marked by a stone tablet in 1916.

When I rectified my Nativity, an. 1647, I found it to be 3 hours 25 minutes 49 seconds a.m. the 4^{qr.} 8 of Ⅱ[1] ascending. But upon Mr. Lilly's [2] rectification thereof, A.D. 1667, he makes the 4^{qr.} 36 Ⅱ ascending. I was baptized the 2nd of June following at St. Mary's Church in Lichfield : [3] my godfathers were Mr. Christopher Baxter, one of the Proctors of the Bishops Court, and Mr. —— Offey, Sacrist of the Cathedral Church.

Before I was carried to church, it was agreed my name should be Thomas (as was my grandfather's). But, when the minister bade name the child, my godfather Offey answered Elias ; at which his partners wondered, and being (at their return home) asked why he so called me, he could render no account, but that it came suddenly into his mind, by a more than ordinary impulse of spirit, my godmother's name was Mrs. Bridges.

When I was about a year old, and set by the fire, I fell into it, and burned the right

---

[1] Ⅱ is the zodiacal sign of the constellation Gemini, and the Twins were adopted by A. as supporters to his coat-of-arms.

[2] WILLIAM LILLY. See p. 27 note.

[3] " ELIAS, sonne of SYMON ASHMOLE was baptised 2nd June 1617." *Church Register*, St. Mary's, Lichfield.

side of my forehead, it resting upon the iron bar of the grate (of which a scar always remained) but my good mother being near, presently took me up, and applied something for my cure.[1]

I had the small-pox (yet but few) as also the swine-pox and the measles, when I was young ; but know not the certain time of either.

Being about 8 or 10 years old (but the year I cannot remember) my mother and I were invited to my cousin Blackburns in Long Parish ; at that time they were building of a barn, and I getting up by ladders to the top thereof, fell down ; in which fall the inside of my right knee struck against the edge of a great beam, which thereby received a deep triangular gash, of which I lay a long time before it was cured.

James Pagit, Esq., sometime Puisne Baron of the Exchequer, married to his second wife, Bridget, one of my mother's sisters, and Widow to —— Moyre a confectioner in London. He had a sister, who first was married to Dr. Masters,[2] Chancellor of

---

[1] The scar is well shown in the engraving of A. by Faithorne cf. p. 54.

[2] ROBERT MASTER, fellow of All Souls College 1590 ; M.P. ; *d.* 1625.

Lichfield ; and after, to Dr. Twisden [1] his successor in the said Chancellorship.

Thomas Pagit his second son (the chief instrument of my future preferment, which I acknowledge with all gratitude to his memory) being much beloved of his Aunt Twisden, came often to Lichfield, when he was young ; whose stay there, as it occasioned an acquaintance with my mother (sister to his mother-in-law) so it begat in him an affection toward me ; insomuch, as having given some good character of me to his father, he became inclined to have me sent to London : And because he and his sons were greatly affected to musick, and very well skilled therein, he was desirous I should spend part of my time at the Music School (having before spent all at the Grammar School) [2] and being competently grounded therein, I became a chorister in the Cathedral Church, where I remained till the said Baron sent for me up to his house.

Mr. Messenger, and after him Mr. Toby Henchman taught me Latin.

[1] CHARLES TWYSDEN, D.C.L., 1618 ; principal of New Inn Hall in Oxford 1618–21.

[2] ADDISON, DAVID GARRICK and DR. JOHNSON were all trained at the Lichfield Grammar School. The choristers were also taught in a picturesque old house which stood till 1772 on the north side of the close. (Humphreys.)

Mr. Michael East, Batchellor of Musick was my tutor for song and

Mr. Henry Hinde, organist of the Cathedral, (he died the 6th of August, 1641 ?), taught me on the virginalls and organ.[1]

1633.

The 2nd of July I began my journey from Lichfield ; my father and mother brought me onward to the far end of Basset's Heath.

The 5th of July, about 11 o'clock before noon, I entred London.

16th July, the before-mentioned Mrs. Twisden died of the *Iliaca Passio*, and was buried the 18th following, in Lichfield Cathedral, in a chappel on the right hand of the Lord Basset's tomb ; where was a monument for Dr. Masters and herself, but broken down by the soldiers in the Parliament War.

4 *Octob.* Mr. John Person a physitian in Coventry (who had married my mother's eldest sister) was buried.

---

[1] A. also learnt to dance. He was taught by Rowland Osborne, and a copy of 'the oulde measures,' written by A. when a boy, is preserved in MS. *Rawlinson* D. 864, f. 39.

1634.

My father died about eleven o'clock before noon.

22. Mr. Symon Martin's letter, which gave me notice of his death, bears date, the 22nd of June.

My father was born upon a Whitsunday in the morning.

He was bred up by his father to his trade ; yet when he came to man's estate, followed it but little : he more affected war than his profession, and spent many of his years abroad, which drew on him a course of expenses and ill husbandry. His first voyage was into Ireland, with Robert Earl of Essex, a °. 159–. Two other voyages he afterwards made, with his son, Robert Earl of Essex into the Palatinate, from whom he received good respect. He was an honest fair conditioned man, and kind to others ; yet through ill husbandry, became a great enemy to himself and poor family.

1635.

In this year I was taught on the harpsichord, by Mr. Farmelow, who lay in St. Michael's churchyard in Cornhill, and

continued learning with him till 31 Jan.
1635–6.

11 *July*. I came to live at Mount
Pleasant, near Barnet, and stayed here the
rest of the summer.

1637.

Aug. 21. I came to Smalewood, to Mr.
Peter Mainwaring's, to ask his consent to
marry his daughter.

Sept. 4. The second time I went to
Smalewood.

16. I returned to London.

1638.

Jan. 23. I came from Mr. Justinian
Pagit.

March 27. I was married to Mrs. Elianor
Mainwaring,[1] eldest daughter to Mr. Peter
Mainwaring, and Jane his wife, of Smale-
wood in Com. Cest. gent. She proved a
virtuous good wife. The marriage was in
St. Benets Church, near Paul's Wharf, by
Mr. Adams, parson there.

[1] Died Dec. 5, 1641.

July 16.   I and my wife went toward her father's in Cheshire, about 4 p.m. where we arrived the 22nd of July.

30. I took possession of my house at Lichfield.

Sept. 10.   My uncle, Thomas Ashmole, caused a Privy Sessions to be called at Lichfield, whereby I had some trouble about my house there : the bill was found *Ignoramus.*

Oct. 8.   I came to London.

In Michaelmas term I began to solicit in Chancery, and had indifferent good practise.

Dec. 20.   I went from London towards Cheshire.

This Term I preferred a Bill in Chancery against my uncle, Thomas Ashmole.

1639.

Jan. 28.   I returned from Smalewood to London.

About the beginning of March, Catherine wife to my brother, Mr. Peter Mainwaring, and one of the daughters and coheirs of Mr. Newton of Pownall in Com. Cest. came to full age.

Mar. 5 p.m. my sister, Ann Mainwaring, was brought to bed of her first child.

In Trinity Term (as I think) I became

acquainted with Dr. Thomas Cademan,[1] the Queen's physitian. About the beginning of July, Peter Venables, Baron of Kinderton,[2] wrote to me, to take upon me the management of his law business.

Aug. 1. I went from London towards Smalewood.

5. I arrived at Smalewood.

Oct. 12. I and my wife returned toward London, beginning our journey from Smalewood this day.

Oct. 20. I began to keep house, being arrived at London, this day.

1640.

Jan. 11. My wife's sister, Mrs. Mary Mainwaring, fell ill of an ague, and having had five fits ;

20. She took her bed.

Feb. 6. 1 p.m. she died. She was buried in the church of St. Clements Danes, near the entrance into the chancel. She had a very handsome funeral, with escutcheons of her arms, in a lozenge, pinned upon her velvet pall.

---

[1] Dr. Thomas Cademan, 1591?–1651, physician to Queen Henrietta Maria ; distiller of strong waters.

[2] Baron Kinderton, a Cheshire lawyer, known as Pet Venables.

18. My cousin, Philip Mainwaring (a younger son of the house of Kerincham) married Mary, the daughter and coheir of Sir John Miller, of Islington.

May 14. Mr. Driver married Mrs. Miller, the other coheir.

April 4. I took lodgings in St. Clement's Lane.

May 19. My wife was brought to bed of a female child, still-born, about noon, which was buried the next day.

June 9. I was entertained by the Lord Keeper Finch,[1] and on the 12th, presented to him upon the recommendation of my worthy friend Dr. Cademan.

Sept. About the beginning of September, my wife fell ill of a fever.

Oct. 31. I removed my study to a chamber in the Middle Temple in Elme Court, lent me by Mr. Thomas Paget.

Dec. 11. Joan Morgan, my maid, died of the small-pox.

1641.

Jan. 18. I began my journey from Smalewood to London.

[1] Sir JOHN FINCH, 1584–1660; Speaker, 1628–40; Baron Finch of Fordwich, 1640–60.

28. I entered London.

Feb. 4. Mr. Hill moved me to an agreement with my uncle, Thomas Ashmole.

Feb. 6. I was admitted of Clements Inn.

Feb. 11. I was sworn an Attorney in the Court of Common Pleas.

April 22. William Clark came to London to be my servant, he continued with me until 1645. 24. He came to dwell with me.

May. About the beginning of May, my maid Elizabeth Coley fell sick of the plague, but escaped.

3. I borrowed of my cousin, Riplingham, £70 and paid it 29 June.

June 21. My brother Mainwaring[1] received £200 from Mr. Simon Ives, upon a mortgage of Smalewood.

22. I was bound with my brother, for performance of covenants, about the beginning of June : towards the end of Trinity Term I was sick for 3 or 4 days.

Aug. 11. I went to Windsor, upon some business for Dr. Cademan, being the first time I saw that Castle.

Sept. 20. I and my wife went toward Smalewood.

23. We came to Lichfield.

---

[1] PETER MAINWARING, see p. 14.

Oct. 12.   My wife quickened.

Oct. 25.   I went towards London, leaving my wife behind me ; because big with child.

29. I came to London.

30. I came to lodge in my chamber at Clements Inn.

Dec. 5.   My dear wife fell suddenly sick about evening, and died (to my own great grief, and the grief of all her friends) ; the next night about nine a'clock she was buried in Astbury Church in Cheshire, near the entrance of the south aisle of that church, viz. the west end of that aisle.

Dec. 14.   I went from London toward Cheshire.

16. Arriving at Lichfield, I first heard of my wife's death.   She was a virtuous, modest, careful, and loving wife, her affection was exceeding great toward me, as was mine to her, which caused us to live so happily together.   Nor was I less beloved and esteemed both by her father and mother, insomuch as at her funeral, her mother sitting near the corpse, with tears, professed to the Baron of Kinderton's Lady (who after told it to me) and others present, that she knew not whether she loved me or her only son better.

18. I came to Smalewood.

1642.

Jan. 16.   I visited my dear wife's grave.

Jan. 18.   I came from Smalewood.

28.   I arrived at London.

Feb. 3.   Mr. Justinian Pagit having proposed to me one of his clerk's places in the Nisi prius office the 10th day of December last ; but finding the terms too hard, I this day resigned it up.

Mar. 7.   I removed my goods to my chamber at Clements Inn, and lay there.

[*June* 18.   Bond of indemnity in which Mr. Ives was concerned.][1]

Aug. 9.   Mr. Hutchinson of Clements Inn, and myself, took a journey, first to see my old schoolmaster, Mr. Henchman, at Drayton in Buckinghamshire, then to Oxford, so into Hampshire, and thence to London.

29.   The troubles in London growing great, I resolved to leave the city and retire into the country, and this day I set forward from London toward Cheshire, to my father-in-law's house at Smalewood.

Nov. 1643.   Sir Thomas Mainwaring, Recorder of Reading, was knighted. I married his widow in 1649.

[1] MS. *Rawlinson* 864.

April 17.   I went toward London with my cousin, Henr. Mainwaring, of Carincham.

25. I came to London.

May 8.   I came from London.

17. I arrived at Smalewood.

July 2.   I went toward Long Witton in Northumberland.

12. I came first to Newcastle with the young Baron of Kinderton.

17. I returned into Cheshire with the Baron of Kinderton's lady.

21. We came into Cheshire.

The rest of the summer I spent at Kinderton, in assisting Mrs. Venables to get off the Baron's sequestration ; but we could not prevail.

Oct. 16.   I went a second journey into the North.

21. I returned toward Cheshire.

1645.

The beginning of this year (as also part of the last) was spent at Oxford by Mr. Hill of Lichfield, and myself, in soliciting the Parliament there against Colonel Bagot, Governor of Lichfield, for opposing the execution of the King's Commission of

Excise (Mr. Hill and myself being Commissioners) whereupon January 8 a letter was sent to fetch the Colonel thither.

Feb. 3. Mr. Hill returned to Lichfield.

Mar. 22. I first became acquainted with Captain Wharton,[1] between eight and nine in the morning.

Apr. 17. Captain Wharton moved me to be one of the four gentlemen of the Ordinance in the garrison of Oxford, 11 a.m.

May 9. I was entered a Gentleman of the Ordinance, 9 a.m.

15. I was affronted by a soldier at my Battery at Dover Pier,[2] but had satisfaction.

Sept. 1. I was very much troubled with my eyes for a week.

14. I christened Mr. Fox his son at Oxford, 4 p.m.

16. Mrs. Henchman died, my schoolmaster's wife.

---

[1] Capt. GEORGE WHARTON sojourned in Oxford in 1633. He seems to have been A.'s first tutor in alchemy and astrology. He was sent to Newgate for satirising Parliament 1647, escaped, recaptured and sentenced to be hung by J. Bradshaw. Ashmole succeeded in obtaining his release, and employed him for a time as estate agent at Bradfield. Like Lilly, Wharton was famous as a maker of Almanacks.

[2] The mound at the east end of Addison's Walk in Magdalen College is named " Dover Pier."

17. This afternoon Sir John Heidon,[1] Lieutenant of the Ordinance, began to exercise my gunners in Maudelin meadows.

Octob. 8. Mr. Wharton was made a Captain of Horse.

12. I first saw Mrs. March in Brazennose Library, being brought thither by Captain Swingfield, 2 p.m. This day Mr. Merick made a motion to me to be a Commissioner of the Excise at Worcester.

Dec. 8. I was recommended to be Commissioner for the Excise at Worcester, unknown to me, which when I knew, I accepted, and prepared for my journey thither.

16. The King caused Mr. —— to be put out of the Commission of Excise, and mine to be inserted in his place.

19. 2 p.m. Mr. Swingfield and my self received the Commission of Excise from the Clerk of the Crown.

21. Sir John Heydon gave me a letter of recommendation to my Lord Ashley[2] at Worcester, of which this is a copy.

---

[1] Sir JOHN HEYDON, royalist lieut.-general of ordnance; "as great a scholar as a soldier especially in mathematics"; *d.* 1657. D.N.B.

[2] ANTHONY ASHLEY COOPER, chancellor of exchequer 1661–72.

My Lord,

This Bearer, one of the Gentlemen of the Ordinance to the Garrison of Oxford, having an Employment in your Lordship's Government, by the Parliament here put upon him. Out of his Desire to be made known and serviceable to your Lordship, hath entreated my Mediation and Attestation, to whose Person, Industry, and Merits, during the Time he hath been interested in his Majesty's Service, under my survey, I can no less than recommend him to your Lordship's favour, as an able, diligent and faithful Man, wherein your Lordship may be pleased to believe,

Your Lordships,

Dec. 21. Most Affectionate Servant,
  1645.   *JOHN HEYDON.*

Dec. 22. I took my journey from Oxford to Worcester. 10 a.m. with Sir Charles Lucas.[1]

23. 8 a.m. I arrived at Worcester.

27. 11.15 a.m. Mr. Jordan, Mayor of Worcester, Mr. Swingfield, and my self, took the oath as Commissioners of Excise in the Town-Hall, and thence went unto the office, and entered upon the execution of the Commission. The Commission bears test the 15th of December preceding.

[1] Royalist defender of Colchester, *d.* 1648.

1646.[1]

Jan. 1. 8 a.m. I delivered Sir John Heydon's letter to my Lord Ashley, who promised me all kindness, and to fix me in the train of Artillery in this Garrison.

3. 3 p.m. Mr. Jordan, the Mayor of Worcester, Mr. Francis Gerard, Mr. John Swingfield, and my self, the three Commissioners of the Excise, being met (at Worcester) Mr. Gerard moved to have me Receiver and Registrar, and Mr. Swingfield to be Comptroller, which was agreed unto.

Jan. 19. I first heard of my mother Mainwaring's death from Mrs. Mary Brereton, my Lord Brereton's daughter.

Mar. 12. 1 p.m. I received my Commission for a captainship in the Lord Ashley's Regiment.

April 18. A new Commission for the Excise came to Worcester.

21. Colonel Baldwin, Mr. Swingfield, and my self, took our oaths to the said Commission, 11.40 a.m.

---

[1] In 1646 A. composed several poems, " A Farewell to a lady going on the water." " The influence of the sun upon nature in summer." " Dreadful apprehensions of the fate of his mistress." " No newes ? not yet ? How lingering are the feete." (MS. *Ashmole* 36.)

27. I was chosen Registrar to the said Commission 1.30 p.m.

28. Mr. Yardley[1] was sworn one of our clerks 3 p.m. upon my recommendation. This Mr. Yardley was one of the choir of Worcester ; after the surrender of the Garrison my servant some years, and upon the King's return, made one of the Gentlemen of his Chapel.

May 19. 5 p.m. Walking in the fields at Worcester, where some were shooting at Rovers, an arrow struck very near me, but I escaped hurt ; thanks be to God.

22. 10 a.m. Sir Ralph Clare[2] moved me to take a command about the Ordinance in the fort of Worcester.

June 12. I entered upon my command as Comptroller of the Ordinance.

18. 1.10 p.m. I received my Commission from Col. Washington.

July 14. Lichfield Close was surrendered to the Parliament.

July 24. Worcester was surrendered, and thence I rid out of town according to the Articles, and went to my father Mainwaring in Cheshire.

July 31. Mr. Richard Harrison, minister

[1] Perhaps father of ELIAS YARDLEY of Reading, p. 37.
[2] Sir RALPH CLARE, 1587–1670, royalist.

of Tetnall formerly, and afterwards of Lichfield, told me of my mother's death,[1] and
that she died about the 8th or 9th of July,
of the plague not long before, that city being
visited this summer. She was a discreet,
sober, provident woman, and with great
patience endured many afflictions. Her
parents had given her exceeding good breed-
ing, and she was excellent at her needle ;
which (my father being improvident) stood
her in great stead. She was competently
read in Divinity, history, and poetry ; and
was continually instilling into my ears such
religious and moral precepts as my younger
years were capable of. Nor did she ever fail
to correct my faults, always adding sharp
reproofs and good lectures to boot. She
was much esteemed of by persons of note
with whom she was acquainted : she lived
in much friendship among her neighbours,
and left a good name behind her. In fine,
she was truly religious and virtuous.

Oct. 16. 4.30 p.m. I was made a Free
Mason [2] at Warrington in Lancashire, with

---

[1] ANNE *née* BOWYER, see p. 7.

[2] It has been stated that A. was " the first Freemason in
England," but this is not the case, for Sir Robert Moray had
been initiated into the Craft at Newcastle five years previously.
The entry is of importance as a proof that Freemasonry had
already ceased to be operative and had become speculative.

Colonel Henry Mainwaring[1] of Karincham in Cheshire ; the names of those that were then at the Lodge, Mr. Richard Penket[2] Warden, Mr. James Collier,[3] Mr. Richard Sankey,[4] Henry Littler, John Ellam, Richard Ellam,[5] and Hugh Brewer.

Oct. 25. I left Cheshire and came to London about the end of this month, viz. the 30th day 4 p.m. About a fortnight or three weeks before I came to London, Mr. Jonas Moore [6] brought and acquainted me with Mr. William Lilly [7] ; it was on a Friday night, and I think the 20th of Nov.

---

[1] Colonel MAINWARING, *b.* 1608, a scion of the younger branch of the Mainwarings of Peover, succeeded to the Karincham estate in 1638.

[2] RICHARD PENKETH, s. of Thomas P. of Penketh Hall, *d.* 1652.

[3] JAMES COLLIER held lands at Newton-le-Willows, *d.* 1674.

[4] RICHARD SANKEY was the father of Edward S., *b.* 1621, who was evidently the copyist of a Sloane Masonic MS.

[5] The ELLAMS were of a yeoman family then long resident in the parish of Winwick, Cheshire.

[6] Sir JONAS MOORE, 1617–79, clerk to Dr. Burghill, chancellor of Durham ; math. tutor to Duke of York, 1647 ; surveyor of Fen drainage system, 1649.

[7] WILLIAM LILLY, 1602–81. Thus began the long friendship that lasted from 1647 until Lilly's death in 1681, when A. placed a monument over his grave, and purchased his library for £50. Lilly evidently made a great impression on Ashmole, for within a year after being introduced to him he wrote a poem " To my worthy Friend, Mr. William Lilly, upon the pub-

Dec. 3. This day, at noon, I first became acquainted with Mr. John Booker.[1]

lishing of his *Christian Astrologie*." He was just recovering from a three months' sickness.

I have read your Booke, and though I crawle
(As the Sicke must doe) behind the Press, and all
That sing your praise in Front ; yet in the Reare
(Rather than not be seen) Let me appeare ;
And tell the World it owes much to your pen,
That has unlockt those cloystered Secrets, when
None else would do't ; teaching us how to read
The mind of Heav'n in English, and not dread
It to be Conjuring; So that by your paines
No room for that black scandall now remaines.
　Th' Worke speakes you Noble, not to hold your Light
Cloyster'd in a darke Lanthorne. 'Tis more bright
'Cause your improved beame, thus shines to all ;
And so communicate's Heroicall.
　You are our English Atlas, you support
Astrologie's fair Credit, and transport
To us, what Aegypt, Greece, Arabia, and
The Eastern world concealed in secret hand,
What they left ravel'd and disorder'd, you
(With happier paines) into this Method drew ;
What they in sev'rall and at tymes enjoy'd
We have in gross at once, and yours beside,
In fine : all theirs, and good ; y' have wisely tooke
Your owne, as th' Essence, does compleate the Booke,
So that till now, (and truly) we may say
Astrologie (to us) in its Chaos lay.

　At A's request in 1670 Lilly was granted a licence to practise medicine by the Archbishop of Canterbury. Five of Lilly's letters are preserved in MS. *Rawlinson* D. 864.

---

[1] JOHN BOOKER, 1603–67, professional astrologer. D.N.B.

22. I was invited by Mrs. March to keep my Christmas with her at Lyme House, which I did.

23. 4.30. I went thither.

1647.

Feb. 10. A boil broke out of my throat, under my right ear.

14. The Mathematical Feast was at the *White Hart* in the old Bailey, where I dined.

Mar. 1. I first moved the Lady Mainwaring,[1] in way of marriage, and received a fair answer though no condescension.

Apr. 14. I went to Sir Arthur Mainwaring's, with the Lady Mainwaring.

May 25. I went toward Bradfield.

27. 8 a.m. Mr. Humphry Stafford[2] and I went into Bradfield House.

June 12. I went from St. James's to Englefield, to table with Antipass Cherving-

---

[1] MARY FORSTER, daughter of Sir WILLIAM FORSTER of Aldermaston was married to four husbands, and died in 1668.

   i. Sir EDWARD STAFFORD of Bradfield, *d.* 1623, leaving a son, HUMPHREY STAFFORD.

   ii. Sir THOMAS MAINWARING, recorder of Reading 1638, *d.* 1646.

   iii. JOHN [THOMAS] HAMLYN, *d.* 1633. (See article by J. C. Smith in *Genealogist*, vol. 29.)

   iv. ELIAS ASHMOLE, as his second wife.

[2] HUMPHREY STAFFORD, son of Sir Edw. Stafford and Mary Forster, who *m.* Ashmole in 1649 as her fourth husband.

ton, and the next morning about 8 a'clock
I came to his house.

14. I first became acquainted with Dr.
Wimberley,[1] Minister of Englefield, 3 p.m.

16. 1 p.m. It pleased God to put me in
mind, that I was now placed in the condition
I always desired, which was, that I might be
enabled to live to my self and studies,
without being forced to take pains for a
livelihood in the world : and seeing I am
thus retired, according to my heart's desire,
I beseech God to bless me in my retirement,
and to prosper my studies, that I may faith-
fully and diligently serve him, and in all
things submit to his will ; and for the peace
and happiness I enjoy (in the midst of bad
times) to render him all humble thanks, and
for what I attain to in the course of my
studies, to give him the glory.

June 25. 11 a.m. The Lady Mainwaring gave me a ring enamelled with black,
whereon was this posie : *A true friend's gift.*

28. 7.15. p.m. I fell ill and 10.30 p.m.
took my bed. I was pained in my head,
reins, thighs, and taking a *Cardus posset* at
night, and sweating upon it, I mended.

---

[1] Dr. GILBERT WIMBERLEY, D.D., Trinity Coll., Cambridge ; canon of Westminster, 1643 ; rector of Englefield,
Berks, 1635 ; *d.* 1653.

July 1. This day I was much pained in my head and eyes.

9. I went to Caversham Lodge to wait upon the King.

12. I went toward London.

23. The Lady Mainwaring entered upon her jointure-lands.

26. 10 a.m. I began to be sick, and 5.15 p.m. I took my bed ; the disease happened to be a violent fever.

30. About 2 p.m. (as I was afterwards told) Mr. Humphry Stafford, the Lady Mainwaring's second son (suspecting I should marry his mother) broke into my chamber, and had like to have killed me, but Christopher Smith [1] withheld him by force ; for which all persons exceedingly blamed him, in regard it was thought I was near death, and knew no body. God be blessed for this deliverance.

Aug. 1. I was in the extremity of my fever, senseless and raging.

14. Being somewhat mended of my fever this day I got up. About this time the Lady Mainwaring fell into a fever, and Captain Wharton [2] had the plague.

---

[1] CHRISTOPHER SMITH, co. Stafford, matr. Queen's Coll., 1628, aged 17 ; rector of Cherington, 1641.

[2] Capt. GEORGE WHARTON, see p. 21.

2 5 was the first day I went down stairs.

3 1. I was very faint and ill again.

Sept. 2. I fell ill again, and became light in my head.

9. I took a purge which wrought very well, and mended.

2 8. I went to visit the Lady Main-waring.

Oct. 26. I fell sick of a Quartan ague, at Mr. Stafford's, having been invited there to dinner.

Nov. 11. I went toward London, and came thither the next day by noon.

2 5. My ague left me.

30. The Lady Mainwaring came to live at her house at Bradfield.

Dec. 16. Being much troubled with phlegm, I took an opening drink from Dr. Wharton.[1]

1648.

Jan. 14. I went toward Bradfield from London.

Feb. 25. I was very ill as I went to Theale.

2 8. Very sick in the afternoon.

---

[1] Dr. THOMAS WHARTON, M.D., 1647 ; the celebrated anatomist of Trinity College, *d*. London, 1673, aged 60.

Mar. 2. Being at Pangbourne, I was very ill there.

12. Captain Wharton taken in his bed 2 a.m.

14. He was carried to Newgate 6 p.m.

May 11. I entertained John Fox into my service.

[*May* 12.] [1]

[1] On May 12 the journey to Bradfield awakened Ashmole's poetic muse, and his Ballad " Vpon my riding post from London to Bradfield 12 May 1648 " is preserved. MS. *Ashmole*, 36 fo. 230 [v].

At foure a Clock this Morne I bid Adieu
To Sack, Chalke, Drawers ; till yᵉ hobnail'd Crew
Of fatt purst Clyentes, to thee (next Tearme) scrape ;
As to a Cuntry Justice coated Ape.
I vs'd nor Prideux warrant, nor his Asses ;
Eight* hard halfe Crownes my warrantes were, and Passes.
My Purse with theis, my Head with Nectar lyn'd :
The Minutes I outstript, left th' Sun behind
Full plum'd my Hatt, my Heeles wing'd for yᵉ Speede ;
I lookt like Mercury on a flying steede.
His Syre was Pegassus, not lymping Gyles,
For in three Howres I scowred thirty Miles.
Whilst a back Winde with its assisting Care,
Wedg'd in my Corpes to cleue the yeilding Aire.
Nor was it strange I posted on soe fast ?
Chanc'ry Clearkes Bills fright Criples into hast.
It was i'th Milkie way I rode, for there
Dazies (like Starrs) bespangled this thick Spheare,
I breath'd perfumed Aire, my horses drew
Ambrosian spirites from this May mornes dew.
The Birdes chirpt Tunes, their nimbler wings did play
Quauer'd Corantes, to shorten the long way.

* Something in shorthand in margin here.

22. The Lady Mainwaring sealed me a lease of the parks at Bradfield,[1] worth ——— per ann.

[30.][2]

The tyme was Tryple, three to one ye hand ;
To their Lavoltes I Gallopt Sarabrand.
My Horses Leggs Division run till they
Came to their Stage ; [a Sembreije rest] and hay,
Where like my Watch I wound, but vp ye Spring
The Ballance plaid againe, th' vnwinding String,
Wheel'd me to my pleas'd Cell : from whence I rest,
  Thyne whilst my owne.   Yet hear'st ? I doe but Jest.

---

[1] The Bradfield estate of Sir Edw. Stafford came to Ashmole by his marriage with Lady Mainwaring.   His notes on the Manor are in MS. *Ashmole*, 1790.

[2] May 30.   A. invited Mr. WILLIAM HUTCHINSON to pay a visit to him at Bradfield.

Why staist thou still in Towne, my Worthy Freind,
And this Vacation in Vexation spend.
Are not the fretting Tearmes enough to give
Thy Toyle, Sweate Labour too : but thou must live
Stand to thy Seate, and Clyents, and in May
When others are reliev'd with ease and play.
For Shame leave Digging with thy Pen : the Plow
Is here left of, and Corn is earring now.
All country pleasures at their full appear
As tempting Invitations that have this heere
Whilst with a pleased Relish I possess
That Nature Wealth which doth this Season blesse.
Twy-light that Natures box of Sweetes enclose
Dayes that are fed with Bloomes, and th' budding Rose
Dews that with Diamonds bedeck the Grasse ;
And every Morning wash the Flowers face
Showers that raine Creame, and winds that Perfumes shed,
Soft gliding Streames, where Troutes in troopes are spred,

June 6. Having entred upon the study
of plants, this day about three a'clock,

Evenings that calmly close with Dewes and Shade
That give Toyle rest, and gently th' Eyes invade
A country where the honest Russet's worne
Whose plain warme Dresse is from their owne Sheepe shorne
Whose food is homely, culed which Labour sweepes
From the pregnant Earth and in a safe coat sleepes,
Whose smiling Feilds and fertill Meadows give
Content and moderate Gaine, by which they Live
Where blooming Maides with harmless ryot play
Away the fagg end a Hollyday.
Whoe to the Bagpipes bow their twisting Hipps
And meete the upstroak with moyst willing Lypps,
That with soft treadings and their ropping Toyle :
Squeeze out Grasse Odors and their sweating Oyle.
Raised more chafed Dust at Barly Breakes
Than th' Graecians did with their Olympique freaks.
That sings and milke, whilst their filld hands keepe tyme
To th' Fidlers Mimmick, Gestures, and his Ryme.
That sweetly sleeps, nor of wich Dreams complaine,
Only their Loves their Hearts, awake, retwyne,
Leaving their Beds when Day begins to peepe
First blesse themselves and next unfold their Sheepe,
Then in their usuall work spend all the Day
Which with their Wheeles goe merrily away.
More I could say t'invite : if this will not,
Dwell still with Stinks, Puggs, and a halfe pint Pott.
From my pleasant Hermitage
This one and thirtyth of my age
Compleate : the Twenty-third of May
Which (as I've heard) was my Birthday.

On another occasion Hutchinson wrote to A., " my wife
thanks you for the orang (a great raritie out of your own
garden), and she is proud of it, and will show it to some bigg-
folk at Aldenh[am] who have orang trees but noe fruit on
them." MS. *Rawlinson*, D 864.

was the first time I went a simpling, Dr. Carter of Reading, and Mr. Watlington,[1] an Apothecary there, accompanying me.

29. The Lady Mainwaring sealed me a lease of Sheffield mead, worth £50 per annum.

Aug. 27. Captain Wharton made an escape out of Newgate.

29. I began my journey toward Bristow, with Mr. Hutchinson.

31. We came to Bristoll.

Sept. 6. We returned to Bradfield.

Oct. 23. Going toward London, I was robbed in Maidenhead Thicket 5.30 p.m.

Nov. 6. Having several times before made application to the Lady Mainwaring, in way of marriage, this day, 11.7 a.m. She promised me not to marry any man, unless my self.

10. 2.15 p.m. She sealed a contract of marriage to me.

15. I was sequestered of my lands in Berkshire.

21. The sequestration was taken off at Reading.

Dec. 5. The Lady Mainwaring was sequestered by the Committee at Reading, upon her son Humfrey Stafford's information.

---

[1] JOHN WATLINGTON, apothecary of Reading.

1649.

Feb. 14. An order for receiving the Lady Mainwaring's rents.

April 7. 11.30 a.m. I came to Mr. Watlington's house to table, who was an apothecary in Reading, and a very good botanist.

25. My journey to the Physick Garden in Oxford.

May 8. I was godfather to Elias Yardly at Reading.

June 3. This afternoon I kissed the Duke of Gloucester [1] and Lady Elizabeth's [2] hands, at Sion House.

Aug. 1. The Astrologers' Feast at Painters-Hall, where I dined.

Oct. 16. I accompanied the Lady Mainwaring to London.

31. The Astrologers' Feast.

Nov. 16. 8 a.m. I married the Lady Mainwaring. We were married in Silver-Street church, London.

20. I was arrested by Mr. Ives for my brother Mainwaring's debt.

---

[1] HENRY, DUKE OF GLOUCESTER, third son of Charles I, 1639–1660.

[2] Lady ELIZABETH, daughter of Charles I, *d.* 1663.

21 Captain Wharton was re-taken and carried to prison.

Dec. 19. I agreed with Mr. Myne,[1] for printing my *Fasciculus Chemicus*.

21. I first began to learn to dissect a body.

1650.

[*Jan.* 23.] [2]

Feb. 18. I met Mr. Ives, and we came to an agreement.

June 3. Mr. Lilly and my self, went to visit Dr. Ardee, at his house in the Minories.

15. My self, my wife, and Dr. Wharton went to visit Mr. John Tredescant,[3] at South-Lambeth.

21. I and my wife went toward Brad-field.

22. 10.30 a.m. We arrived there.

24. Mr. William Forster [4] and his lady came to visit us.

25. I and Captain Wharton went to visit him at Rushall.

---

[1] RICHARD MYNNE, 1628–50.

[2] A's letter to A. Dee in MS. *Ashmole* 1790.

[3] JOHN TRADESCANT, the younger, 1608–62, the Virginian traveller and collector ; bestowed his famous collection on Ashmole, who presented it to Oxford.

[4] Sir WILLIAM FORSTER of Aldermaston was the father of A's second wife.

26. 9.42 p.m.   We arrived at London.

July 2. 6 p.m.   I was served with a subpœna at Sir Humfrey Forster's [1] suit.

29. Much troubled with the toothache on my right side.

Aug. 8.   I being at the Astrologers' Feast, 2 p.m. I was chosen Steward for the following year.

Captain Wharton having been carried to the Gate-House the 21st of November last ; the next day after, I went to Mr. Lilly, and acquainted him therewith, who professed himself very sorry, because he knew Bradshaw [2] intended to hang him ; and most generously (forgetting the quarrels that had been between the Captain and him) promised me to use his interest with Mr. Bulstrode Whitlock [3] (his patron) to obtain his release. I thought it not prudent to have my name then (as the times stood) to appear in print, as the instrument that wrought Mr. Lilly to do this kindness for him ; and therefore in Captain Wharton's Epistle to the Reader before his Almanack, in 1651, wherein his public acknowledgments are

---

[1] Sir HUMPHREY FORSTER was uncle to Charles Stafford.

[2] RICHARD BRADSHAW.   D.N.B.

[3] BULSTRODE WHITELOCKE, matr. St. John's coll. 1620 ; M.P. Staffs. 1626 ; patron of Lilly ; speaker 1656 ; *d.* 1676.

made, of Mr. Lilly's assistance in this
strait, all acknowledgments to me are
omitted, tho' in truth, I was the only person
that moved and induced, and constantly
solicited Mr. Lilly to perfect his enlarge-
ment.   Having at all times, since my return
to London, anno 1646, befriended Captain
Wharton, not only in discovering all designs
that I heard were laid against him, either at
Mr. Lilly's or elsewhere ; but also affording
him my purse freely and liberally, toward
his support in many necessitous occasions.
Upon Mr. Lilly's application to Mr. Whitlock, he advised that the Captain should lie
quiet, without making the least complaint,
and after Christmas, when his being a
prisoner was almost forgotten, Bradshaw
out of the way, and Mr. Whitlock Chairman
to the Council of State ; (Mr. Lilly having
also by this time, made some other of the
said Council, the Captain's friends) upon his
petition he was discharged, no other engage-
ment being taken from him but that he
would not thenceforward write against the
Parliament or State.   Hereupon he became
utterly void of all subsistence (which whilst
he was under troubles, some or other contri-
buted unto, besides what he got by writing
against those times) and thereupon, consult-

ing with me, about a new course of life, and
how he might subsist, I frankly offered him
my house at Bradfield in Berks, for him, his
wife and family, to live at, with some other
advantages there ; which he most gladly and
thankfully accepting, he went thither, and
passed his time with quiet and comfort for the
most part, till his Majesty was restored to
his Crown ; and hereupon he styled me in
his Almanack for the year 1653, his Oaken
Friend.

Aug. 13. I bought of Mr. Milborne all
his books and mathematical instruments.

14. 8.30 p.m. I bought Mr. Hawkins's
books.

Oct. 18. I put in a plea and demurrer
to Sir Humfrey Forster's bill.

Nov. 1. My cousin Bridget Smart
(only daughter to my uncle Anthony Bowyer) [1] was buried.

12. I agreed with Mr. Lyster for his
house in Blackfriars, where I afterwards
dwelt.

23. 2 p.m. He sealed me a lease of the
said house at £44 per annum.

26. p.m. I came thither to dwell.

---

[1] ANTHONY BOWYER matr. Ch. Ch. 1650 ; M.P. Southwark
1685–7 ; *d*. 1709, aged 76.

1651.

Jan. 1. I fell into a great looseness, which turned into a fever, but mended next day.

7. Captain Wharton returned from Bradfield, whether I sent him to receive my rents.

16. 4 p.m. My demurrer against Sir Humfrey Forster's bill was argued and held good.

22. About this time my left side of my neck began to break forth, occasioned by shaving my beard with a bad razor.

27. About this time I grew melancholy and dull, and heavy in my limbs and back.

About this time I began to learn sealgraving, casting in sand, and goldsmith's work.

Feb. 1. 3.30 p.m. I agreed with Mrs. Backhouse of London, for her deceased husband's books.

Mar. 7. I went to Maidstone with Dr. Child the physician. And 3 p.m. I first became acquainted with Dr. Flood.

18. This night my maid's bed was on fire, but I rose quickly (and thanks to God) quenched it.

---

[1] Dr. LEWIN FLUDD, created M.D. Padua 1639, incorporated at Oxford 1661.

April 3. p.m.   Mr. William Backhouse [1]
of Swallowfield in Com. Berks, caused me
to call him Father thenceforward.

[1] WILLIAM BACKHOUSE matr. Ch. Ch. 1610–11 aged 17 ;
inherited Swallowfield from his brother Sir John Backhouse
in 1649 ; "a most renowned chemist and Rosicrucian and a
great encourager of those who studied chemistry and astrology" (A. Wood) ; *d.* 30 May 1662. His daughter Flower
became successively Mrs. W. Bishop, Lady Wm. Backhouse
and Countess of Clarendon, and retained her father's friendship for Ashmole, see p. 134.

A ballad to "my worthily honoured William Backhouse,
Esq., upon his adopting me to be his son." MS. *Ashmole*
36 ff. 241ᵛ, 242.

> From this blest Minute I'le begin to date
> My Yeares and Happiness ; (since you create
> What wise philosophers call Lyfe ;) and vow
> I ne're perceiv'd what Being was till now.
>   See how the power of your Adoption can
> Transmute imperfect Nature to be Man.
> Nay, with one Worde may yet refine it more,
> Than all the best digested Indian Oare.
>   Your Son ! 'Tis soe ! For I begin to finde,
> Your Auncestor's large Thoughts grow in my Minde,
> I feel that noble Blood spring in my Heart,
> Which dose intytle me to some small parte
> Of grand sire Hermes' wealth, and hope to have
> Interest in all the Legacies he gave
> To his successive Children, from whom too
> I most derive what is conferr'd by you.
> To prove each mie descent, I need not see
> A byast Herrald for my pedigree ;
> That I'm true bred, question it he that dare,
> If these my Aeglite eyes on th' sun can stare
> Or cause a Mercury in Crest I hold
> Since my crude Mercury's transmute to gold.

D

26. 5.30 p.m. My Father Backhouse brought me acquainted with the Lord Ruthin,[1] who was a most ingenious person .

June 10. Mr. Backhouse told me I must now needs be his son, because he had communicated so many secrets to me.

July 21. I gave Mr. Grismond[2] my *Theatrum Chemicum Britanicum*[3] to print.

I'll vouch my Fate for Honour, Witt, Descent,
And all, which to th' Hermetick Tribe is lent.
Then be you blest, my Starrs, who gave to me
So blest a time for this Nativity,
That plac'd the golden Lyon in the East
When Sol within the Ram, the Nynth possesst,
As if their Influence meant to ope the way,
To make Night misteries shine clear as day.
Hast yee some good directions that shall lead
My Father's hand with that of Blessing to me Heade,
And leave it there.   His Leaves of Hermes tree
To deck the naked Ash bequeath to me
His Legacy of Eyes to th' blinde Mole spare
And (though a younger Son) make me his Heire.

---

[1] Sir THOMAS RUTHVEN of Freeland N.B., created a baron by Charles II in 1651, was a great chemist.

[2] JOHN GRISMOND II, printer.

[3] A's second alchemical work, published in 1652, was a collection of old medico-philosophical writings.   The following passages in the preface are of interest :

" Our English Philosophers generally, (like Prophets) have received little honour (unlesse what hath beene privately paid them) in their owne Countrey ; nor have they done any mighty Workes amongst us, except in covertly administering their Medicine to a few Sick, and healing them. . . .   But in

Aug. 11. Captain Wharton went to receive my rents at Bradfield.

Aug. 14. The Astrologers' Feast at Painters Hall, London.

This night about one a'clock, I fell ill of a surfeit, occasioned by drinking water after venison. I was greatly oppressed in my stomach ; and next day Mr. Saunders the astrologian sent me a piece of bryony root to hold in my hand, and within a quarter of an hour, my stomach was freed of that great oppression, which nothing which I took from Dr. Wharton could do before.

Parts abroad they have found more noble Reception, and the world greedy of obteyning their Workes."

"My Annotations are limited within the Bond of what is Historical, or what occasionally must needs intrench on the Confines of other Arts, and all glosses upon the Philosophicall Worke purposely omitted."

" May the *God of Nature* be gratiously pleased (out of the Immense Treasury of his Goodness) to vouchsafe all such (whose good Angells direct them to, or have already Religiously Engaged them in this mysterious knowledge) the Full and Entire Accomplishments of a True and Pious Philosopher, [To wit, Learning, Humility, Judgement, Courage, Hope, Patience, Discretion, Charity and Secrecie :] That so they may enjoy the Fruits of their Labours, which otherwise will be in vain, and unpleasant : and causelessly render the Divine Service and Secret it selfe, Contemptible."

Several of A's Alchemical and astrological notes made about 1651–2 are preserved in MS. *Rawlinson*, D 864.

About this time my brother Peter Mainwaring's [1] wife died.

Sept. 11. Captain Wharton went to receive my rents.

22. Mr. Vaughan began to engrave the pictures in Norton's Ordinal, he wrought and finished all the cuts for my *Theatrum Chemicum Britanicum*, at my house in Blackfriars.

30. Captain Wharton arrested, I and Mr. Grismond, bail.

Oct. 9. My Father Backus and I went to see Mr. Goodier, [2] the great botanist, at Petersfield.

20. Mr. Lilly gave me several old astrological manuscripts.

Nov. 10. About 4 p.m. my wife's eldest son, Mr. Edward Stafford, died.

11. 10 p.m. He was buried in Bradfield Church.

12. Sir John Backus [3] of Swallowfield, his widow died.

Dec. 7. 2 p.m. Dr. Pagit lent me several chymical manuscripts, and here began my acquaintance with him.

---

[1] MAINWARING, see p. 14.

[2] JOHN GOODYER, 1592–1664, the eminent Hampshire botanist. See Gunther *Early British Botanists*.

[3] Sir JOHN BACKHOUSE of Swallowfield, 1626–49.

19. I sent Captain Wharton to receive my rents at Bradfield.

1652.

Jan. 21. The gum at the back end of the right side of my upper jaw cleft, and about 9 p.m. I felt a new tooth coming up.

26. 6 p.m. The first copy of my *Theatrum Chemicum Britanicum*[1] was sold to the Earl of Pembroke.[2]

29. 10 a.m. Mr. Lilly gave me his picture in oil colours, of which there never had been copy taken.[3]

Feb. 11. 2.45 p.m. The statute of £3000 and Mr. Stafford's counterpart of his lease of my wife's jointure was delivered to me, by direction of Sir Arthur Mainwaring's lady, who had been trusted with it.

About this time I began to learn Hebrew of Rabbi Solomon Frank.

Mar. 1. I fell sick of the headache and a cold. This sickness continued five weeks.

---

[1] A's notes for the *Theatrum* all contained in MS. *Ashmole* 971. The original imprimatur is dated 21 March, 1650–1.

[2] PHILIP HERBERT, 1619–69, 5th Earl of Pembroke, councillor for Trade and Navigation 1660.

[3] This portrait dated 1646 has unfortunately been removed from the Old Ashmolean Building, where A. willed it to hang. It is described by Poole, *Cat. of Oxford Portraits.*

8. 6.15 a.m. Dr. Wharton let me blood.

10. This morning my Father Backhouse opened himself very freely, touching the great secret.

April 9. I paid my man John Fox his wages, and discharged him of my service.

12. This morning I received more satisfaction from my Father Backhouse, to the questions I proposed.

I sent Captain Wharton to Bradfield to receive my rents.

27. I went to the sessions at Newbury, where Colonel Evelin, Governor of Wallingford (being set on by Sir Humfrey Forster) was exceeding bitter against me, to the wonder of the whole Court. ♌ in the ascendent all the while.

May 28. The inquisition upon my statute of £3000 pounds was found at Maidenhead.

I and my wife tabled this summer at Mr. Tredescant's.

June 14. 11 a.m. Dr. Wilkins [1] and Mr. Wren [2] came to visit me at Blackfriars, this was the first time I saw the doctor.

---

[1] JOHN WILKINS, 1614–72, warden of Wadham College 1648–59 ; convener of meeting at which the Royal Society was founded.

[2] Sir CHRISTOPHER WREN, 1632–1723, professor of astronomy at Gresham College 1657–61.

23. Captain Wharton was sent to receive my rents, and July 16 brought his wife and family to Bradfield.

Aug. 2. I went to Maidstone Assizes to hear the witches tried, and took Mr. Tredescant with me.

16. I went toward Cheshire.

26. Dr. Wharton fell sick of a violent and dangerous fever about noon.

28. I arrived at Gawsworth,[1] where my father-in-law, Mr. Mainwaring, then lived.

Sept. 11. Young John Tredescant died.

15. He was buried in Lambeth church-yard by his grandfather.

23. I took a journey into the Peak, in search of plants, and other curiosities.

27. I came to Mr. Jo. Tompson, who dwelt near Dove Bridge ; he used a call, and had responses in a soft voice. He told me Dr. Wharton was recovering from his sickness, and so it proved.

Oct. 2. I came to Lichfield.

3. Mr. Anthony Diot [2] moved me to refer controversy between me and my uncle, Thomas Ashmole.

13. My said uncle quitted his title to me,

---

[1] Near Macclesfield.

[2] ANTHONY DYOTT matric. Corpus Christi coll. aged 17 ; M.P. for Lichfield 1604–11 ; father of Richard, p. 108.

which pretended to my house in Lichfield,
and sealed to me a deed of bargain and sale.

14. He also sealed me a release, and gave
me possession.

Nov. 2. 4 p.m. I returned to London,
and in an hour after to my house.

3. Mr. Lilly called before the Committee
of plundered ministers, and committed.

20. My wife went again to Mr. Tredescant's, to stay some time there.

21. I discharged my man Hobs of my
service.

Dec. 14. I was served with a subpœna
at Sir Humphrey Forster's suit, 3.40 p.m.

15. His bill was filed.

18. My sister, Mrs. Dorothy Mainwaring,
came to live with my wife, 11 a.m.

She stayed with her but till the 16th of
January following.

1653.

Jan. 13. I held a Court at Bradfield, as
Lord of that Manor.

Mr. Anthony Barker of Sunning was my
steward; Sir Humfrey Forster coming thither
I arrested him.

17. My wife left Mr. Tredescant's, and
came to Mr. Flint's.

Mar. 18. The Astrologers' Feast was held.

April 8. Dr. Langbaine,[1] Provost of Queen's College, showed me Mr. Selden's [2] letter to him, wherein he said, he should be glad to be acquainted with me ; for he found by what I had published, that I was affected to the furtherance of all good learning.

20. This morning I first became acquainted with Arise Evans,[3] a Welsh prophet; and speaking of the Parliament, I asked him when it would end ? He answered, the time was short, and it was even at the door; this very morning at eleven a'clock, the Mace was taken away from the Speaker, and the Parliament dissolved ; and I conjecture it was much about the time that Arise Evans and I had this discourse.

May 12. 3 p.m. My cousin, William Ashmole, came to London.

---

[1] Dr. GERARD LANGBAINE matr. Queen's 1628, aged 19 ; provost 1645–†1657-8.

[2] JOHN SELDEN, M.P. Oxford 1640–53 ; keeper of records in Tower 1643 ; *d.* 1654.

[3] ARISE EVANS, *b.* 1607, fanatic, declared himself to be Christ 1647. He " had a fungous nose, and said it was reveal'd to him, that the King's hand would cure him ; and at the first coming of King Charles II in St. James's Park, he kiss'd the King's hand, and rubb'd his nose with it, which disturbed the King but cured him." Aubrey, *Miscellanies.*

13. He went to Mr. Sidley[1] upon trial.

My Father Backhouse lying sick in Fleet-Street, over against St. Dunstan's Church ; and not knowing whether he should live or die, about eleven a'clock told me in syllables the true matter of the Philosopher's Stone, which he bequeathed to me as a legacy.

June 21.   I agreed with Dr. Bathurst[2] for the remaining years, in my house at Blackfriars.

July 25. 9.30.   I was first acquainted with Mr. Selden, who used me very courteously, and encouraged me in my studies.

Aug. 8. 8.30 a.m.   I began my voyage with Dr. Cunn into Cornwall, he going thither to open a mine for the Lord Morne.

17. 9 p.m.   We came to Boconock.

Sept. 12. 9.15 p.m.   We returned to London.

Oct. 1. 7 p.m.   I first became acquainted with Mr. Ogilby.[3]

4. I was much troubled with the toothache, Major Ruswell (Dr. Bathurst's apothecary) stopped it.

---

[1] Sir CHARLES SEDLEY.

[2] Dr. JOHN BATHURST, 1607–59, physician to Cromwell.

[3] JOHN OGILBY, 1600–76 ; cosmographer to Charles II.

16. Sir John Heydon, Lieutenant of the Ordnance to King Charles the 1st, and my worthy friend, died.

Nov. 18.   My aunt Bowyer, wife to my uncle Anthony Bowyer, was buried.

20. I was again troubled with the tooth-ache for three days.

23. My good friend and neighbour Dr. Wimberley, minister of Englefield [1] in Berkshire, died.

25. He was buried at St. Margaret's Westminster, where formerly he had been parson.

This day I bound my cousin William Ashmole an apprentice to a saddler, Mr. Clothier.

1654.

Jan. 21.   Doctor Wharton began his lecture at the Physicians' College 10 a.m.

Feb. 6.   The hearing in Chancery (came on), wherein Sir Humphrey Forster was plaintiff against me.   As soon as my answer was opened, it was referred to Mr. Chaloner Chute [2] my counsel to determine.

---

[1] Englefield 6 miles west of Reading and 2 miles from Bradfield, the home of Sir T. Mainwaring's widow.

[2] CHALONER CHUTE, Speaker, bought the Vyne 1653, *d.* 1659.

Mar. 11. 4 p.m. Mr. Chute signed his award.

16. In pursuance whereof I received from Sir Humphrey Forster £350. 11 a.m.

Feb. 2. I acquainted Doctor Wharton with my secret for the cure of the *Iliaca Passio*, and he applied it this morning to Mr. Faithorne [1] the graver, and it cured him.

July 3. My wife went to lodge at Mr. Wittes.

17. I came to Lichfield.

22. I returned thence.

[*Aug.* 19.] [2]

22. Astrologers' Feast.

24. I made a journey to Canterbury, Dover, etc.

Sept. 1. I returned to London.

15. I went (to) visit Mr. Oughtred, [3] the famous mathematician.

28. I received £300 more from Sir Humphrey Forster.

Oct. 7. Mr. William Floyd's [4] first wife

[1] WILLIAM FAITHORNE, the elder, 1616–91. See p. 9.

[2] 1655 Aug. 19. " Came to see me Sir E. Hales, Mr. Ashmole . . ." Evelyn, *Diary*.

[3] WILLIAM OUGHTRED, 1575–1660, mathematician.

[4] Dr. WILLIAM FLOYD, 1637–1710, presented to rectory of Bradfield by Ashmole 1654 ; Bishop of Norwich 1685–1709.

(was) buried at Swallowfield[1] in Berk-shire.

Nov. 24. 6 p.m. My good father-in-law, Mr. Peter Mainwaring, died at Gaws-worth.

Dec. 8. Doctor Pordage[2] (was) put out of Bradfield living : by his removal it fell to me to present, and knowing the worth and learning of Mr. Floyd (then living with my Father Backhouse as tutor to his children) I resolved to bestow it upon him, and there-upon sent for him up to London, and on the 18th acquainted him with my intention.

30. I signed a presentation to him ; he was examined by the Triers, and passed with approbation : but designs being laid against him by Mr. Fowler[3] and Mr. Ford, both ministers of Reading, who endeavoured to bring in Doctor Temple, supposing Sir Humphrey Forster had right of presentation,

[1] Swallowfield, the seat of the Backhouse family, is 5 miles S. of Reading. JOSEPH BLAGRAVE, nephew of John Bla-grave, also lived there and belonged to the " astrologers' circle."

[2] JOHN PORDAGE, 1607–81, formerly Vicar of St. Lawrence in Reading, had quarrelled with the vicar of St. Mary's, Reading, Christopher Fowler, who roused local feeling against Pordage's belief in " spooks " and effected his eviction.

[3] CHRISTOPHER FOWLER, vicar of St. Mary's, Reading. D.N.B.

he thought better to resign his presentation to me, than to undergo a contest with those men.

1655.

[*Jan.* 12. A. wrote to ask Booker to meet him and Lilly " at the Maire maid "]. *MS. Ashmole* 385.

[*Feb.* 22][1]

Mar. 22. 6.45 p.m.   I subscribed my last receipt to Sir Humphrey Forster in full of £700 given me by Mr. Chute's award. £100 of this money I gave to my son Mr. Edward Stafford's widow, who had no jointure settled on her, and was in great want.

30.   Hereupon I presented one Mr. Adams, who, having a living of £140 per ann. and finding he must undergo a contest with those that opposed Mr. Floyd, thought fitter to keep his own living, than part with it in hopes of a far better.

June 16.   Captain Wharton was taken prisoner at Bradfield, and 18th, carried to Windsor Castle.

---

[1] A. wrote to EDWARD SHERBURN about the solar eclipse—a " double ecclips " of clouds.   MS. *Ashmole* 423.

19. 10 a.m. A letter from the Lord Commissioners of the Great Seal was left at my lodging, to appear at my wife's suit, who sued me for alimony.

Aug. 7. Captain Wharton came home upon his parole.

29. I signed and sealed my presentation for Bradfield living to Mr. Lancelot Smith 6.15 a.m. and delivered it to the Committee. This man, after some contest, enjoyed the living ; and the right of presentation being acknowledged to be mine, I had no farther trouble.

This day the Astrologers' Feast was held.

Nov. 28. The Peace between England and France was proclaimed at Westminster 10.45 a.m., and at 11.45 it was proclaimed at White-Hall.

1656.[1]

[12 *Jan.*][2]

Apr. 17. Archbishop of Armagh (was) buried.

May 23. First show at Sir William Davenant's opera.[3]

[1] In this year A. helped to catalogue the Tradescant Collection with the collaboration of George Wharton.

[2] A's letter to ALESTREY is in MS. *Ashmole*, 1439.

[3] Sir WILLIAM DAVENANT at Lincoln coll. c. 1620 ; knighted 1643 ; originator of " opera " in England 1656.

June 26. I fell sick, and had a great looseness.

July. In this month I was troubled with a great pain in my right breast.

12. I paid Mr. Faithorne £7 for engraving my picture.

Aug. 1. Journey to Mr. Sterill's in Essex.

Sept. 4. Cousin —— Thompson [1] (was) christened.

11. I went toward Lichfield.

13. About 9 a.m. I came first to Mr. Dugdale's at Blyth-Hall. [2]

Oct 9. I returned to London 12.30 p.m.

Dec. 19. I went toward Blyth-Hall.

1657.

Jan. 14. 10.40 a.m. I returned to London.

Feb. 22. My cousin Everard Mainwaring died.

Mar. 27. I went toward Blyth-Hall.

Apr. 20.[3] 5 p.m. I bruised my great toe with a fall of a great form.

[1] WILLIAM TOMPSON mentioned in A's will, p. 151.

[2] Sir WILLIAM DUGDALE, 1605–86 ; proclaimed Charles II at Coleshill 1660 ; Garter King of Arms 1677.

[3] 1657, Apr. 20. A. wrote a letter to Dugdale on his exploration of the Roman road " Bennevanna " from Weedon to Lichfield. It is printed in Dugdale's *Life*.

May 2. 7 a.m. I returned to London.

19. I accompanied Mr. Dugdale in his journey toward the Fens. 4.30 a.m.

19 from London to Puckridge. 10 a.m.
    to Cambridge. 10 p.m.

20 to Audrey Causey. 3 p.m.
    to Eriff. 4.30 p.m.
    to Mr. Hamonde of Wilberton. 7.30 p.m.

21 to Ely. 10 a.m.
    to Mr. Moores at Southery. 6 p.m.

22 to Sr. Ralfe Skipwith. 9.40 a.m.
    to Derham Abbey. 11 a.m.
    to Salthern load. 4 p.m.
    to Mr. Ed. Barber. 4 p.m.

23 to Outwell. 10.30 a.m.
    to Laurence Oxborow Esq. at Hackbech Hall. 2 p.m.
    to Lynn. 7 p.m.

25 to Wisbech. 7 p.m.

26 to M. Patons at Doddington. 5.30 p.m

27 to Withesey. 1 p.m.
    to Peterborow.

28 to Thorp ye Lo: Cheife Justice St. John. 9.30 a.m.
    to Spalding. 8 p.m.

29 to Boston.

30 to Lincolne.   1 p.m.

   to Mr. Dodsworthe at Burton.   7 p.m.

June 1 to Gainsborow.   6 p.m.

  2 to Selby.   4.30 p.m.

  3 to Yorke.   9.30 a.m.

  4 to Pomfract at noone.

   to Rotheram.

  5 to Derby

  6 to Blyth Hall.   4.30 p.m.

July 7. 6.45 a.m.   I returned to London.

Sept. 22.   I fell ill of the toothache, which continued three days.

Oct. 8.   The cause between me and my wife was heard, where Mr. Serjeant Maynard[1] observed to the Court that there were 800 sheets of depositions on my wife's part, and not one word proved against me of using her ill, nor ever giving her a bad or provoking word.

9. The Lords Commissioners having found no cause for allowing my wife alimony, did 4 p.m. deliver my wife to me ; whereupon I carried her to Mr. Lilly's, and there took lodgings for us both.

Nov. 11. 2.15 p.m.   I was admitted of the Middle Temple.

Dec. 1.   About 10.30 p.m. it thundered

---

[1] Serjeant JOHN MAYNARD, 1602–90.   D.N.B.

and lightened, and at this time was the writ sealed for summons to the new Lords of the Parliament.

22. I and my wife came toward Albury.

28. I went to London.

29. And thence toward Blyth-Hall.

1658.[1]

Jan. 15. I came to Bradfield.

19. I returned to Albury.

Mar. 30. I dined with the Florida Ambassador at Mr. Martin Noel's.

May 7. I first went to the Record-Office in the Tower, to collect materials for my work of the Garter.

9. I was struck by a coach-horse, on the inside of my left thigh.

June 12. I first became acquainted with Sir Roger Twisden.[2]

July 2. Was the Antiquaries' Feast.

[3][3]

---

[1] A's treatise on the Philosopher's Stone, with Faithorne's portrait of the author, was published in 1658, and in the same year JONAS MOORE gave A. an urn from the Fens.

[2] Sir ROGER TWISDEN, 1597–1672. D.N.B.

[3] " 1658, July 3. To London, and dined with Mr. Henshaw, Mr. Dorell and Mr. Ashmole, founder of the Oxford repository of rarities "—Evelyn, *Diary*. The concluding note must have been added by Evelyn in 1683 or later.

27. 4 p.m. I went toward Warwick-shire and Staffordshire. In this journey I visited Sir Thomas Leigh,[1] Sir Harvey Bagot,[2] Sir Richard Lewson,[3] (and) the Earl of Denbigh.[4]

[28. "Some observacons taken concerning Watling streete how it beares." MS. *Ashmole*, 784, f.11.]

Aug. 21. I returned to London.

Sept. 8. I went toward Oxford.

10. I began to make a description of the coins in the Archives there.

25. I returned to London, from Oxford.

Oct. 2. Mr. John Watlington, Apothecary of Reading, and an able botanist (my very good friend), was buried.

5. Mr. Lilly received a gold chain from the King of Sweden.

Nov. 2 was the Astrologers' Feast.

13. I was entered into Mr. Henshaw's[5]

---

[1] Sir THOMAS LEIGH of co. Warw., matr. Magd. coll. 1608 ; cre. Baron Leigh 1643 ; *d.* 1671.

[2] Sir HERVEY BAGOT of Blithfield co. Staff., matr. Trinity 1608, aged 18 ; cre. baronet 1627 ; M.P. Stafford 1640 ; *d.* 27 Dec. 1660.

[3] Sir RICHARD LEVESON, matr. Queen's 1617, aged 19 ; M.P. Salop 1626 ; *d.* 1661.

[4] BASIL FEILDING, Earl Denbigh, *d.* 1674.

[5] THOMAS HENSHAW, matric. Univ. coll. 1634, aged 17 ; gentleman of privy chamber to Charles II ; F.R.S. 1663 ; *d.* 1699, aged 82. D.N.B.

Chamber in the Middle Temple, which I bought of him for £130, being admitted to it this day 7.30 a.m.

17. 11.15 a.m. I brought my goods thither, and 2 a.m. came the rest.

1659.

May 24. I became acquainted with Mr. Scipio Squire.

25. I went to Windsor, and took Mr. Hollar[1] with me to take views of the Castle &c.

Aug. 16. I came to Roe-Barnes, to table there.

21. My study was broken open by the soldiers, upon pretence of searching for the King, but I lost nothing out of it.

Dec. 12. Mr. Tredescant and his wife told me they had been long considering upon whom to bestow their closet of Rarities when they died, and at last had resolved to give it unto me.

14. This afternoon they gave their scrivener instructions to draw a deed of gift of the said closet to me.

16. 5.30 p.m. Mr. Tredescant and his

---

[1] WENCESLAUS HOLLAR, 1607–77, engraved at least 2733 prints.

wife sealed and delivered to me the deed of gift of all his Rarities.

1660.

Jan. 3. My uncle Anthony Bowyer died.

Mar. 2. I went into Warwickshire.

Apr. 11. I returned to London.

June 6. 4.15 p.m. I first became acquainted with Sir Edward Walker Garter.[1]

16. 4 p.m. I first kissed the King's hand, being introduced by Mr. Thomas Chiffinch.[2]

18. 10 a.m. Was the second time I had the honour to discourse with the King, and then he gave me the place of Windsor Herald.

22. The warrant bears date 22 June.

About this time the King appointed me to make a description of his medals,[3] and I had them delivered into my hands, and Henry the VIIIth's closet assigned for my use.

July 19. This morning Mr. Secretary

[1] Sir EDWARD WALKER, Garter King of Arms 1644 ; *d.* 1676.

[2] THOMAS CHIFFINCH, 1600–66, keeper of the Jewels 1660.

[3] A's work on the King's medals was commemorated by the casket in J. Riley's portrait.

Moris [1] told me that the King had a great kindness for me.

Aug. 6. Mr. Ayton, the King's chief gentleman-usher, came to me in the closet, and told me, the King had commanded that I should have my diet at the waiters' table, which I accordingly had.

10. 6.30 p.m. The Officers of Arms took their oaths, and my self among them, as Windsor Herald.

14. This afternoon was the first public meeting of the Officers of Arms in the Herald's Office.

21. I presented the King with the three books I had printed, viz. *Fasciculus Chemicus*, *Theatrum Chemicum Britanicum*, and *The Way to Bliss*.

27. This day the Monument of Capt. —— which stood on the left hand of the north dore in Westminster Abbey, was broken downe by boyes and other people.

Sept. 1. This afternoon after Dinner the Duke of Gloucester fell sick of the small pocks.

3. About 11 o'clock my warrant signed for the Comptroller's Office in the Excise.

4. This morning his Majesty signed

---

[1] Sir WILLIAM MORICE, 1602–76, secretary of state 1660–8.

another warrant for me, for the Auditors place in the Excise.

[10][1]

14. This day I began to search the Scottish Records, being appointed thereunto with Mr. Dugdale, Mr. Ryley, etc., by his Majesty before they be sent back to that Kingdom.

17. I delivered my said warrant to the Commissioners of Appeals for the Excise.

18. This afternoon I attended the Committee of Appeals with his Majesty's warrant to invest me in the Comptroller's place of the Excise.

27. This day Mr. Secretary Morrice moved the King for my Precedency above Mr. Henry St. George, Mr. Tho. Lee, and Mr. Thomas St. George, which his Majesty was graciously pleased to grant in regard I had the first grant from him after his arrival in England, before them that made greater speed to get their patents under seal than I did. Upon which motion the King was

---

[1] A. was made a Commissioner to examine Hugh Peters, who had obtained the King's Library during the rebellion and had sent valuable curiosities abroad all over Europe. His copy of the King's warrant, dated 10 Sept. 1660, authorising him to examine Hugh Peters concerning royal books and medals embezzled, is in MS. *Rawlinson*, D 864.

pleased to use this expression that I was a person greatly deserving, and he had a particular kindness for me.

29. This evening I had my warrant signed by the King for the precedency in the Herald's Office, as also a warrant to the Lord Treasurer to admit me into the Comptroller's place of Excise. Prince Rupert also arrived at London.

Oct. 9. This evening about 7 o'clock Sir Alan Broderick made me acquainted with the Lord Chancellor.

12. This morning I showed the King the young children which Dr. Warner had preserved. The one was a male infant about 4 months, who was cut out of a woman's belly in Covent Garden (she dying of a consumption) and had been (now four years past) luted up in a glass, and preserved by a liquor of his preparation from putrefaccon, the flesh not so much as rumpled, but plump as it was when taken out of ye wombe. The other was 2 girls joyned together by the breast and belly (which monster was borne about the king's coming in), they were dryed, and preserved with spices.

Prince Rupert brought some ladies into my closet at Whitehall that morning after, to see them.

I carried them also to the Princes Royall.

About 9 o'clock I acquainted the King with my discovery of Irish lands, whose gracious answer was that what I desired should be done.

13. This day about 11 o'clock I brought Dr. Warner to the King, who kist his Majesty's hand, and presented him with an antique gold ring, wherein was a sapphire, and in it a head cut of one of the younger Constantines. His Majesty gave him thanks for this piece of antiquity, and commended very much his invencon of the liquor that had preserved the above monstrous child.

19. The King signed my warrant whereby he admitted me Comptroller of the Excise. Whereupon the next day I attended the court of the Excise to give me my oath. They desired that the Committee of Appeals might join with them ; and on the 24th of Oct. following, both Committees meeting and debating the matter of the oath, concluded that it was in neither of their powers to administer any oath, because the oath appointed for the first Comptroller, seemed not to be appointed for his successors, nor could it be given (nor myself take it) without some alterations which they could not take

upon them to alter ; and thereupon it was thought I might execute the office without an oath, until the parliament took care to prescribe one.

24. 5 p.m. I came to the Excise-Office and took possession of the Comptroller's Office[1] [in Broad Street].

29. I entered upon execution of this Office. This morning about 9 o'clock Mr. Bartlet resigned his Comptrolership of the Excise to me.

30. My warrant for precedency in the Herald's Office was read by Sir Edward Walker, Garter, in Chapter. About 10 a'clock in the morning the Queen-Mother landed at Dover.

Nov. 1. This day was kept solemnly at the Middle Temple and after the auncient manner. The Lord Chancellor, Judges and Sergeants that were of the Society dined in

---

[1] " 24 October. So to Mr. Lilly's with Mr. Spong, where well received, there being a clubb to-night among his friends. Among the rest Esquire Ashmole, who I found a very ingenious gentleman. With him we two sang afterwards in Mr. Lilly's study. That done, we all parted, and I home by coach, taking Mr. Booker with me, who did tell me a good many fooleries which may be done by nativities, and blaming Mr. Lilly for writing to please his friends and to keep in with the times and not according to the rules of art, by which he could not well erre, as he had done." Pepys, *Diary.*

the Hall, after dinner they had a play, viz.
Witt without Money. This night about 7
a'clock was the Duke of Somerset buryed.

2. 6 p.m. The Queen-Mother landed at
Whitehall. Prince Edward landed there at
that tyme also.

7. 30 min. p.m. I took the oath of
supremacy (upon my admittance to the
bar) in the Middle Temple Hall. About
4 p.m. the Queen-Mother and the Princess
Henrietta Maria, came into my closet at
Whitehall.

2. I was this night called to the Bar
in the Middle Temple Hall.

7. I had my admittance to the Bar, in the
said Hall.

Dec. 1. About 1.15 p.m. I moved the
King in the proposals for advance of his
customs, 60,000 per annum, and acquainted
him with several inconveniences and dis-
advantages if he farmed either the Customs
or the Excise. Whereupon he was pleased
to say he had no mind to farm them. He
gave me a gracious audience, and among
other things told me, he believed I was an
honest man. He lookt upon me as an honest
man, and would take care for me as an
honest man.

13. The King going to a Play at the

new Theatre this afternoon, had his coach (the leathers whereby the coach hung broke and so the coach fell from the wheels) over-turned over against the new Exchange, but (blessed be God) had no hurt. Sir Francis Floyd passing by took him in his arms and carried him to his coach. The Earl of Latherdale and my Lord of Ossory being with the King in his coach.

20. This morning it was rumoured at Whitehall that the Princess Royal was fallen sick of the small pox.

24. About noon this day the Princess Royal dyed.

25. This morning was the first tyme I waited on the King to Chapel in my Herald's coat.

Dec. 28. I took my oath as Comptroller of the Excise before Baron Turner.

1661.

Jan. 1. About 3.30 p.m. The Duke of York's eldest son was christened. . . .

2. This afternoon I was voted into the Royal[1] Society at Gresham College.

[1] The word 'royal' was added later. The Society was hardly entitled to be called " Royal " before the date of its Charter of Incorporation on 15 July 1662. A. was proposed as a candidate on Dec. 26, 1660.

5. This night the Duke of York and his Duchess first lay together in Whitehall.

9. This afternoon I went to take my place among the royall [1] Society at Gresham College.

15. I was admitted into the Royal Society at Gresham College.

[15] [2]

Feb. 9. Warrant (was) signed by the King for my being Secretary of Surinam in the West-Indies [and to hold during my life].

Mar. 9. This day about 11 o'clock the proclamacon for the Coronacon was proclaimed at Whitehall Gate, after at Westminster, next at Chancery Lane and then in Cheapside and lastly at the Exchange about one o'clock. First rode the Serjeant Trumpeter with his Mace, after him followed 16 trumpets and a kettle drum, who sounded all the way by turns. After these I rode with a Serjeant at Arms on my left hand, next Mr. Ryley with another Serjeant at Arms, and lastly Mr. Owen (who proclaimed

---

[1] The word 'royall' was added later.

[2] Sir EDWARD NICHOLAS, 1593–1669, private secretary to Charles II, received or wrote a letter dated 15 Jan. 1661, recommending A. as Comptroller of the Excise.

the proclamation) between two serjeants at arms.[1]

Apr. 3.　My Patent for Comptrollership of the Excise, bears test.

13.　The King gave my Lord Chamberlain order to settle me as the first Herald, in case any dispute should happen.

May 16.　The Grant of Arms to me from Sir Edward Bysh [2] Clarencieux bears date.

[23] [3]

June 28.　John Walsh was sworn my deputy.

July 6.　Mr. Thomas Chiffinch dined at my Chamber in the Middle Temple.

Nov. 12.　I christened Mr. Butler the goldsmith's son, William

1662.

Jan. 26.　I paid in £50 the half of my royal present to the King.

Mar. 15.　I sent a set of services and

---

[1] End of MS. *Ashmole*, 826.

[2] Sir EDWARD BYSSHE, 1615?–1679, Garter King of Arms 1646–60.

[3] 23 May. A. sat next to Pepys at dinner at the Lord Mayor's, " I had very good discourse with Mr. Ashmole, wherein he did assure me that frogs and many insects do often fall from the sky ready formed." Pepys, *Diary.*

anthems to Lichfield Cathedral, they cost me £16.[1]

Apr. 22. Mr. John Tredescant died. [*May* 13][2]

29. I was made one of the Commissioners for recovering the King's goods.

30. My Father Backhouse died this evening at Swallowfield.

This Easter-Term I preferred a Bill in Chancery against Mrs. Tredescant, for the Rarities her husband had settled on me.

June 17. About 3 p.m. The Commissioners for the office of Earl-Marshal first sat in Whitehall.

This afternoon my Father Backhouse was buried, in Swallowfield Church.

29. 11.30 a.m. I first kissed the Queen's hand.[3]

Aug. I accompanied Mr. Dugdale in his Visitation of Derby and Nottingham shires.

---

[1] Copy of letter dated 15 March 1661–2 from A. to sub-chanter of Lichfield on presenting 12 vols. of church services and anthems with his arms impressed thereon. MS. *Rawlinson*, D 864. Another copy in MS. *Ashmole*, 1523.

[2] 1662, 13 May. Hamet, the Morocco Ambassador " was entertained at Oxford, and, about the same time, dined with Elias Ashmole, who made him a present of a magnifying glass." Evelyn, *Diary*.

[3] CATHARINE OF BRAGANZA *m.* Charles II, 20 May, 1662.

9. I bought Mr. Turnepennies interest in the lease of Homerich lands.[1]

Sept. I paid the other half of my royal present to the King, viz. £50.

Dec. 5. I christened Captain Wharton's daughter Anne.

1663.

Mar. I accompanied Mr. Dugdale in his Visitations of Staffordshire[2] and Derbyshire.

May. Toward the end of this month I christened Mr. Timothy Eman's son of Windsor.

27. I fell ill of a feverish distemper.

July 6. I went toward Oxford, attending the body of Archbishop Juxon.[3]

Aug. 3. 9 a.m. I began my journey to accompany Mr. Dugdale in his Visitation of Shropshire and Cheshire.

Oct. 10. I returned to London.

---

[1] ZACHARY TURNEPENNY, sub-chanter of Lichfield, to whom A. wrote on 3 May 1662. MS. *Ashmole*, 1521.

[2] A's notes made on this Visitation are preserved in MS. *Rylands*, e 27.

[3] WILLIAM JUXON matric St. John's 1602 ; archbishop of Canterbury 1660 ; *d.* 1663. At the funeral of Archbishop Juxon in Oxford " Mr. Elias Ashmole, Windsor herald, carried the crozier star." (Wood.)

F

Nov. 21. Mr. Povey[1] brought the Earl of Peterborough[2] to my Chamber.

1664.

Jan. 19. Mr. Thomas first promised me a place in the White-Office.

Feb. 5. The Benchers of the Middle Temple granted me an assignment of my Chamber in the Middle Temple.

8. My picture (was) drawn by Mr. Le Neve[3] in my Heralds Coat.

9. I gave £20 toward repair of Lichfield Minster.

12. Mr Dugdale fell sick of a fever.

Mar. 17. I christened Secundus, son to Mr. Lacy the Player.[4]

May 18. My cause came to hearing in the Chancery against Mrs. Tredescant [before Lord Chancellor Clarendon].

June 17. I gave five volumes of Mr. Dugdale's works to the Temple-Library, (and had this acknowledgment)

[1] ? JOHN POVEY, matr. Trinity 1635 ; chief justice in Ireland 1673.

[2] HENRY MORDAUNT 2nd earl of Peterborough 1624?–1697.

[3] Sir WILLIAM LE NEVE *b. c.* 1600 ; *d.* 1661. York herald 1625 ; Norroy 1633 ; Clarenceux 1635 ; declared lunatic in 1658.

[4] JOHN LACY, the comedian, see Aubrey *Lives*.

Parliamentum tentum 17th *die Junii* 1664.

Ordered that Mr. Ashmole *of the outter Bar have their Masterships Thanks for the Books now presented by him to their Masterships for the Library.*

27. The White Office was opened, wherein I was Comptroller.

July 16. I having bought the third part of my Chamber upon the death of Mr. Parrot, the Bench this day gave me an assignment of it.

Aug. 9. Grand day at the reading in the Middle Temple, whereat I was one of the stewards.

1665.

Feb. 8, about 8 a.m. Mr. Thomas (gave) a warrant of attorney to confess a judgment to me of £1200.

17. Sir Edward Bish sealed his deputation to me for visiting Berkshire.

Mar. 11. I began to make my Visitation of Berkshire at Reading.[1]

30. I ended my Visitation at Windsor.

[1] On May 11 of the year of the Plague, Ashmole as Windsor Herald started out to make a Visitation of Berkshire, beginning at Reading, and noting pedigrees, arms and antiquities, beginning the *History and Antiquities of Berkshire*. His survey of

Aug. 26.   I went toward Blyth-Hall.

About 15 of July (the Plague increasing) I retired to Roe-Barnes, and the following winter composed a good part of my work of the Garter there.

1666.

Jan. 17.   I bestowed on the bailiffs of Lichfield a large chased silver bowl and cover, cost me £23 8s. 6d.[1]

June.   I presented the public Library at Oxford with three folio volumes, containing a description of the consular and imperial coines there, which I had formerly made and digested, being all fairly transcribed with my own hand.   (In acknowledgment of which the following was entered in the register of benefactors.

Elias Afhmole *armiger, & Regius Fecialis de* Windefore, *vir præftantiffimus & rei antiquariæ peritiffimus, accuratiffimum anti-*

1664–1666 is included in MS. 850 and was printed in three octavo volumes entitled *The History and Antiquities of Berkshire.* London 1719.   Reprinted 1723, and at Reading in 1736.   The original manuscript is contained in MSS. *Ashmole* 850, 851, 852.

[1] The Letter of thanks of the Corporation of Lichfield is printed on p. 155.

*quorum Numismatum Laudentium Catalogum
in tria Volumina distributum concinnavit, &
Bibliothecæ Bodleianæ dono dedit.*[1]

Aug. I went to Blyth-Hall, and returned
the same month.[2]

Sept. 2. The dreadful fire of London
began.

Oct. 4. 1.30 p.m. Some of my books
carried to my cousin Moyre's, were returned
to my Chamber at the Temple.

11. 1.30 p.m. My first boatful of books,
which were carried to Mrs. Tredescant's
3rd of September, were brought back to
the Temple.

18. 4 p.m. All the rest of my things
were brought thence to the Temple.

1667.

May 21. I bought Mr. John Booker's
study of books, and gave £140 for them.[3]

---

[1] The Preface to the Laudian Catalogue is printed with
Dr. Barlow's belated letter of thanks on pp. 159–165.

[2] 1666 Aug. 3. " Returned with Mr. A. to Blyth Hall."
Dugdale *Diary.*

[3] JOHN BOOKER died in 1667. " His library of books "
according to a note by his friend Lilly " came short of the
world's approbation and were by his widow sold to Elias
Ashmole, Esq., who most generously gave her far more
money than they were worth : but out of his respects unto

[*June.*] [1]
July 16. I went toward Warwickshire.
24. I returned to London.
31. I went again toward Warwickshire.
Aug. 21. I returned to Roe-Barnes.
Nov. 25. I took a lease of the Moggs 9
Nov. in Lichfield from the bailiffs, and
this day paid £20 in part of £40 fine.

1668.

Jan. 11. I paid to Mr. Rawlins £20
the remaining part of my fine for the
Moggs at Lichfield.
April 1. 2 a.m. The Lady Mainwaring,
my wife, died.
25. Mr. Joseph Williamson [2] and Dr.
Thomas Smith [3] (afterwards Bishop of Carlisle) dined with me at my Chamber in the
Temple.

the deceased and his memory, he most willingly paid her the
money."—" They cost me forty pounds." Ashmole's note
to the above statement.

---

[1] On June 14, 1667, Anthony Wood went from Oxford up
to London in the stage-coach, and on Sunday June 16 he
went to the Middle Temple, and found out Mr. Dugdale in
the apartment belonging to Elias Ashmole.

[2] Sir JOSEPH WILLIAMSON matr. Queen's 1650 ; P.R.S. ;
d. 1701.

[3] THOMAS SMITH, 1615–1702, chaplain to Charles II.

June 9. 5 p.m. The Lords Commissioners of the Treasury appointed me to execute the Office of Accomptant-General in the Excise and Country Accomptant.

15. 5 p.m. They appointed me also to execute the place of Country-Accomptant in the Excise.

Aug. 10. I went toward Blyth-Hall.

[24]¹

26. I returned to London.

Sept. 4. 7.30 a.m. I concluded with Mr. Laurence, for his house in Sheere-Lane. At 7 p.m. he sealed his assignment to me.

16. Doctor Currer, the Chemical Physician, my most entire friend, died.

Oct. 1. He was buried at St. Clements Danes, Dr. William Floyd preached his Funeral Sermon, November 1.

Nov. 3. I married Mrs. Elizabeth Dugdale, daughter to William Dugdale, Esq., Norroy King of Arms, at Lincoln's Inn Chapel. Dr. William Floyd married us, and her father gave her. The wedding was finished at 10 p.m.

Dec. 3. Doctor William Floyd married.

29. Justinian Pagit, Esq., died.

---

¹ 1668 Aug. 24. "Paid to A. 40*s*. which he laid out for me."—Dugdale, *Diary.*

1669.

Jan. 2. Mr. Just. Pagit buried at St. Giles's in the Fields.

April 15. Mr. Rose, the King's gardener, and my self, went to Mrs. Tredescant's, and thence to Captain Forster's at South-Lambeth, where I first was acquainted with him.

17. Mr. Oldenburgh (Secretary to the Royal Society) sent me a letter, that Count Magalotti would visit me at my Chamber, from the Prince of Tuscany.

19. Count Magalotti and two other gentlemen of the Prince of Tuscany's chief attendants, came to my Chamber to see my library and coins.

27. I felt the first touch of the gout, in my great toe, on my left foot, and in my left forefinger.

June 5. I and my wife went to Hersham to visit Mr. Lilly.

14. We returned to London.

July 6. I went toward Oxford.[1]

---

[1] "July 6, T., Elias Ashmole, Esq., came to Oxon to spend some time there, and to see the solemnity of the great Act approaching. He lodged at the Greyhound Inn without the East-Gate of Oxon, and then he very kindly sent of A. W. to come to him, purposely to deliver commendations to him from his father-in-law Will. Dugdale, Norroy K. of Armes. He continued in Oxon 7 or 8 dayes and A. W. attended him

9. The possession of the theatre (built by Dr. Sheldon,[1] Archbishop of Canterbury) was taken by the Vice-Chancellor.

I received the honour of being made Doctor of Physic at Oxford.[2]

Aug. 11. I and my wife went again to Mr. Lilly's.

22. Sir William Backhouse of Swallowfield died.

Sept. 3. I returned to London from Mr. Lilly's.

Mrs. Dorcas Pagit, wife to Justinian Pagit, Esq., was buried.

21. I went toward Swallowfield to serve at the funeral of Sir William Backhouse.

27. I let a lease of Homerich Lands[3] to H. Aldridge for seven years.

every day in seeing many curiosities, as the painting in Alls. coll. chappel, the paynting in Magd. coll. chappell, and the paynting in the Theater. They were often in the Physick Garden with Jacob Bobart the keeper (an old acquaintances of Mr. Ashmole), who shewd them many choice plants, herbs, grafts and other curiosities, to Mr. Ashmole's great content." (Wood.)

---

[1] GILBERT SHELDON, 1598–1677, warden of All Souls 1626–48, and '59 ; archbishop of Canterbury 1663–77.

[2] The Diploma MS. *Ashmole* 1000 is reproduced in *Early Science in Oxford*, iii. p. 304.

[3] At Homerich, now Hammerwich, is a farm recently in occupation of a collateral descendant, Elias Ashmall. (Wood.)

28. He was buried at Swallowfield.[1]

Nov. 8. This evening Dr. Yates,[2] Principal of Brazen-Nose presented me with a Diploma [3] from the University of Oxford, for my degree of Doctor of Physic between six and seven at night.

About the middle of December, my friendship began to be renewed with Dr. Wharton,[4] which had been discontinued for many years ; by reason of his unhandsome and unfriendly dealing with me.

1670.

Mar. 14. I bestowed a grave-stone on Mr. Booker formerly, and this day paid for it ; (it had this inscription in capital letters).

---

[1] 1669. Sept. 28. Ashmole as Windsor Herald, assisted by Henry Dethick Rouge Croix, and Francis Sandford Rouge Dragon, directed the funeral of Sir William Backhouse who had died on Aug. 22nd, leaving his widow, Dame Flower, nine adventurer's shares in the New River Company.

[2] THOMAS YATE, D.D. ; principal of Brasenose Coll. 1660.

[3] " Oct. 30, S. [In convocation.] E. Ashmole who had had his grace granted for Dr. of Phys. 19 Aug., 1669, supplicated for to be diplomated, because being full of business, he could not come to be presented : his diploma was dated and sealed in Congregation T. 2 Nov. 1669." (Wood.)

[4] See p. 32, note.

Ne oblivione contereretur Urna
Johannis Bookeri *Astrologi,*
qui fatis cessit
VI*to Idus* Aprilis, *Anno Christi Juliano*
MDCLXVII.
Hoc illi posuit amoris Monumentum
Elias Ashmole
Armiger.

16. I was entertained by Monsieur Lionberg, the Swedish Envoy.[1]

31. I obtained the King's warrant to my Book of the Garter.

[*May* 1.] [2]

5. The Earl of Anglesea [3] visited me at my Chamber in the Temple.

10. I dined at Sir Charles Cotterel's [4] with the Danish Envoy,[5] and after dinner they went to my Chamber in the Temple ; where

[1] W. B. LEYONBERGH whose letter to A. dated 10 May, 1671, is in MS. *Ashmole,* 1131.

[2] " May 1, Sn., dined with Mr. Ashmole at his house in Sheer-lane, neare Temple barr ; and John Davis of Kidwelly was there. After dinner he conducted A. W. to his lodging in the Middle Temple, where he shewed him all his rarities, viz. antient coines, medalls, pictures, old MSS. etc., which took them up neare two hours time." (Wood.)

[3] ARTHUR ANNESLEY, 1st Earl of Anglesea, 1614–86.

[4] Sir CHARLES COTTEREL, D.C.L., 1670 ; master of the ceremonies ; knighted at Oxford after Edgehill 1644.

[5] CHRISTOFFE LINDENOW agent for King of Denmark wrote to A. 6 Dec. 1670. MS. *Ashmole,* 1131.

I so satisfied the Envoy touching the King of Sweden's precedence in the Order, before his masters ; that he thereupon waved the further prosecution of that affair.

June 22. Captain Burgh,[1] my old acquaintance, died.

July 5. The Lord Hatton,[2] my much honoured friend, died this morning.

I fell ill of a surfeit, but thanks be to God, I recovered the next day.

9. I dined with the Swedish Envoy.[3]

27. Sir Gilbert Talbot,[4] Master of the Jewel House, and Mr. Joseph Williamson dined at my Chamber in the Temple.

Aug. 19. 6 p.m. My cousin Moyre of Totenham, died.[5]

24. My self and wife went to Captain Wharton's, at Greenwich.

Sept. 25. 11.30 a.m. I became acquainted with the Count de Monroux,[6] Envoy from the Duke of Savoy.

---

[1] A. bequeathed his portrait to be placed in the Museum.

[2] CHRISTOPHER HATTON, 1605–70, succeeded by his son Christopher in 1670.

[3] Vide p. 85.

[4] Sir GILBERT TALBOTT matr. Ch. Ch. 1626 ; F.R.S. ; master of Jewel office to Charles II ; *d.* 1695.

[5] MOYRE. See p. 9.

[6] His letter to A. dated Turin, 24 June, 1673, is in MS. *Ashmole*, 1131.

Oct. 8. I moved my Lord Archbishop of Canterbury[1] for a licence for Mr. Lilly, to practise physic, which he granted.

[*Oct.* 18.][2]

[*Oct.* 19.][3]

Nov. 18. I fell ill of the gout, in my great toe on the right foot.

20. I bled with leeches, and was well the next morning.

1671.

Jan. 9. My sister Dugdale died.

Mar. 13. I became acquainted with Mr. Peter Arnold the chemist.

---

[1] ARCHBISHOP SHELDON.

[2] Oct. 18. According to a memorandum pasted in Ashmole's own copy of his book in Oxford, he was visited by a Livonian knight, NICHOLAS VON VILCEN.

" *Generose et nobilissime Domine, adfuerunt hic duo nobiles Germania, artis chymicae amatores, qui viderunt et legerunt librum Dominationis Vestrae Theatrum chimicum Britannicum, quaedam cum Dominatione Vestra communicaturi, si grave non est et hora commoda designabitur. Commorantur in S. Steevens alle (St. Stephen's Alley), at the* 3 *glasses of Mumm. Nicholas von Vilcen, Eques Livonus,* 18 *Oct.* 1670."

[3] 1670 Oct. 19. FLOWER, Lady BACKHOUSE, aged 29, was married by Dr. Lloyd to Henry Hyde, Viscount Cornbury, eldest son of the great Earl of Clarendon. Through this marriage Flower became sister-in-law to James II, and aunt to Queens Mary and Anne.

April 4. My brother Dugdale married to Mrs. Pigeon.[1]

May 16. I let a lease of my house in Lichfield, to Mr. Edmund Falkingham, for seven years.

July 20. I went toward Blyth-Hall with my wife.

31. I came to Lichfield.

Aug. 10. I and my wife went to Lichfield, where we were entertained by the Bailiffs at a dinner, and a great banquet.

15. We went to the Earl of Denbigh's at Newnham.

18. 4 p.m. I arrived at London.

Sept. 21. I went again toward Blyth Hall.

Oct. 5. I came to Lichfield, where I met my brother Mainwaring.

16. I and my wife returned to London.

19. My brother Mainwaring came to London.

Dec. 7. My brother Mainwaring took his oath, as one of my deputies, so did Mr. Street.

1672.

Jan. 24. I was entertained at dinner by the Venetian Agent.

---

[1] Sir W. DUGDALE's son m. ii Mrs. E. Pidgeon, da. of Thos. Pidgeon, Alderman of Coventry.

May 8. 2.40 p.m. I presented my Book of the Garter to the King.[1]

[*July* 6.] [2]

20. I and my wife went to Mr. Lilly's, where we stayed till September the 2nd.

Aug. 20. My good friend Mr. Wale sent me Dr. Dee's [3] original books and papers.

---

[1] A sumptuous folio of eight hundred pages illustrated by Hollar.

[2] On July 6, 1672 Wood received from E. Ashmole, Esq., his book entitled *The Institutions, Lawes and Ceremonies of the noble Order of the Garter*, and sent in return a letter of thanks for the present, and afterwards his *Hist. et Antiq. Un v. Oxon.* when finisht. Wood's letter is still preserved in MS. *Ashmole* 1131 f. 281 and is dated 16 July 1672. A long correspondence between A. and Wood followed. Eighteen letters of A's to Wood, mostly dated 1672 to 1674, are in MS. *Wood* F. 39, ff. 57–96.

[3] ARTHUR DEE, alchemist, son of Dr. John Dee, was born in 1579. In 1621 he accompanied the Ambassador Isaac Ivanovitch Pogosheff to Moscow where he became physician to the Czar. Ashmole's first work, the *Fasciculus Chemicus* was a translation of a Dee's work composed in Latin in Moscow. The complete title is *Fasciculus chemicus abstrusae hermeticae scientiae, ingressum, progessum, coronidem, verbis apertissimis, explicans ex selectissimis et celeberrimis authoribus, tali serie collectus et depositus, ut non modo huius artis tyronibus sed candidatis, summo emolumento, instar speculi Philosophiae habectur, a nemine hac methodo distributus, opera et studio Arthuri Dee, Archiatri Magni Imperatoris totius Russiae."*

The preface to the reader is dated *Ex Musaeo nostro, Moscuae, Kalend. Martii* 1629." It was published at Basle in 1629 and then in 1631 at Paris, and finally translated into English by Ælias Ashmole, whose name was anagrammatized into 'James Hasolle'. See p. 130, note.

ELIAS ashmole

Sept. 14. The Earl of Peterborough having about June, by the Duke of York's command, called at my Chamber in the Temple, for one of my Books of the Garter, to carry to the Duke, then at sea ; he this day told me the Duke received it with much pleasure, and (the Earl) believed he had read it all over.

27. Mr. Philip Floyd's Patent passed the Great Seal for the reversion of my office of Comptroller of the Excise.

Oct. 12. 10.30 a.m. I sprained my right foot.

17.[1] The Earl of Peterborough presented me to the Duke of York,[2] who told me he had read a great part of my book, that I had done a great deal of honour to the Order of the Garter, that I had taken a great deal of pains therein ; and deserved encouragement 9.20 a.m.

[*Dec*. 14.] [3]

---

[1] A. wrote to Sir Edw. Walker.—MS. *Ashmole*, 1131.

[2] The king's brother afterwards James II. " His Royall Highness the Duke of Yorke was pleased to represent to the Sovereigne, that Elias Ashmole, Esq., Windsor Herald had lately with great industry and expence composed and published a large book in folio. . . ."

[3] London 14 Dec. 1672. " Mr. Davenport is ready to serve you." . . . " Mr. Blount passing through Oxford has promised to tell you that Dr. John Dee was of Cambridge." Letter from A. to Wood.—MS. *Wood* F, 39.

17. Being at the Treasury Chamber, the Lord Treasurer Clifford[1] very courteously invited me to his lodgings in the Court.

20. I waited on him, and was received with great kindness.

23. The Earl of Bristol[2] gave great commendations of my book, and said he thought the Knights of the Garter were obliged to present me with some considerable gift, and that himself would move it.

[30.][3]

1673.

Jan. 11. This evening I sat with the Lord Treasurer two hours.

[11.][4]

27. 10.40 a.m. The Earl of Bedford gave his approbation, with great commendation of my book of the Garter.

---

[1] THOMAS CLIFFORD, Lord Treasurer in 1672, *d.* 1673.

[2] GEORGE DIGBY 2nd Earl of Bristol, 1612–77.

[3] 30 Dec. 1672. Dee's biography is worthy of being made "a particular worke." Cf. the copy of Sir T. Browne's MS. on Dec. dated, March 1654.—MS. *Wood* F, 39.

[4] 11 Jan. 1672–3. "Dr. Yates can give you the best account of my admittance into Brazenose Collidge wch I think I was in 1645. He entred my name in the House Booke: but I cannot tell you of what house my father Dugdale was admitted of: when he comes up you shall know. All hearty services to Dr. Yates, Dr. Barlow, your good selfe, etc. I am, Yor reall and affectionate friend, E. ASHMOLE." Letter from A. to Wood.—MS. *Wood* F, 39.

Feb. 3. 10.30 a.m. I delivered my petition to the Earl of Arlington,[1] for the Custom of Paper, with desire of his opinion about it : he answered, it was but a reasonable request, and (he) would confer with the Lord Treasurer about it, before he moved the King, and that he would do me service. [8.][2]

13. 8.20 p.m. I moved the Lord Treasurer for the arrears of my pension, as Windsor Herald, and to favour my petition for getting the Custom of some paper ; the first he said should be done, and to the second, he would be my friend, and so he was.

Mar. 13. My Book of the Garter sent to Captain Bartie to be presented to the King of Denmark.[3]

[15.][4]

16. I grew indisposed with a fulness in my stomach, but taking some physic, I grew well.

[1] HENRY BENNET 1st Earl of Arlington 1618–85. Lord Chamberlain 1674.

[2] 8 Feb. 1672–3. A. wrote to Wood about L. Noel and Dugdale, " who M.A. Oxon *c.* 1644 ; yet was not adm. of any College."—MS. *Wood* F, 39.

[3] CHRISTIAN V, King of Denmark.

[4] 15 Mar. '72. " Search for account of Mr. Lawrence Noell at Lincoln's Inn."—MS. *Wood* F, 39.

A. wrote to Th. Henshaw on the same day.—MS. *Ashmole*, 1131.

25. The Earl of Denbigh came to my house to visit me.

April 2. 7 p.m. Coming from Windsor in a coach with Sir Edward Walker, the coach overturned, and I sprained my left wrist.

17. I delivered my Book of the Garter to Sir John Finch,[1] to present it to the Duke of Tuscany.[2]

May 24. I received the Lord Treasurer's warrant for £106 13s. 4d., the arrears of my pension.

June 18. I received my Privy-Seal for £400 out of the Custom of Paper, which the King was pleased to bestow upon me, for my work of the Garter.

21. I tooke my leave of the late Lord Treasurer.

29. I was let blood.

July 4. The learned and ingenious Sir Robert Murrey[3] died.

[23.][4]

Sept. 29. I renewed my lease of Homerich lands from the Vicars of Lichfield.

---

[1] Sir JOHN FINCH, F.R.S., 1663 ; ambassador to Constantinople 1672 ; *d.* 1682.

[2] COSMO, Duke of Tuscany, had visited Oxford in 1669.

[3] Sir ROBERT MORAY, F.R.S., † 1673.

[4] Date of letter from A. to Sir J. Williamson.—MS. *Ashmole*, 1131.

Oct. 4. 2.15. I and my wife came from Hersham to London, having spent a good part of the summer with Mr. Lilly.

12. The Lady Forster, Sir Humfrey Forster's widow, died.

[21.] [1]

Nov. 8. This morning Dr. Wharton was found almost dead in his bed of an apoplexy, and palsy on his left side.

12. He sent for me at midnight, and because some differences had formerly fallen out between us, he desired to be reconciled to me, which he was.

15. 1.15 a.m. Dr. Wharton died, and was buried in Baringshaw Church in a vault.

Dec. 3. Dr. Tern the Physician, died this evening : he was buried at St. Andrew's Undershaft, the seventh of January following.

[9.] [2]

1674.

[*Jan.* 19.] [3]

---

[1] 21 Oct. 1673. Letter from A. to Wood. On Sir E. Hoby, of Bysham and Dr. W. James, Bp. of Durham.—MS. *Wood* F. 39.

[2] 9 Dec. 1673. Letter from A. to Wood. Mr. Dodsworth dyed in August 1654. Dugdale asks for evidence of W. of Waynflete being set down as Lord Chancellor of England. Respects to Provost of Queens.—MS. *Wood* F, 39.

[3] Letter to Sir J. Williamson in MS. *Ashmole*, 1131.

Feb. 25. 9.30 a.m.   I desired Mr. Hayes, the Earl Marshal's Secretary, to move his Lord to give me leave to resign my Herald's place.

[*Mar*. 21.][1]

April 2.   Earl Marshal came to see my Chamber at the Temple.

13. He gave me a George in gold, which his grandfather wore, when he went Ambassador into Germany.

24. My wife and I went to Mr. Lilly's, where we stayed till 8 September following.

May 29.   About 5 p.m. the order was made in the Chapter House at Windsor, for recommending me to the Knights of the Garter.

[*June* 17.][2]

20.   I dined with the Duke of Lauder-

---

[1] 21 Mar. 1673-4. Letter from A. to Wood.   " Having now by me Mr. Allen's Copy of the 2nd and 3rd Bookes of Ptolomies Quadripartite. It was bestowed on me by Mr. Lilly the 3rd of May 1652.   And one of the two coppies, transcribed from the originall, wch Sir Thomas Alisbury had of the guift of Mr. Allen ; the other Coppy M. Huniades (the great Chimist) had.   The title is thus . . ."—MS. *Wood* F, 39.

[2] 17 June 1674. Letter from A. to Wood.   Advises Wood to dedicate his book to the King.—MS. *Wood* F, 39.

" The King of Denmark has sent me a gold chaine and medall worth 8*oli*. "

dale[1] at Ham, whither he had invited me, and treated me very kindly.

July 1. Sir John Davis,[2] sometime of Pangborne in Berkshire, died.

20. I met with Mr. Thomas Henshaw upon his return from Denmark, having brought me a gold chain, and that King's medal thereat, from the said King.

27. I first spake with the Prince Elector of Brandenburgh's Envoy.[3]

Aug. 1. I lent Mr. Edward Hopkins £400, upon a mortgage of his lands in Little Pipe near Lichfield.

4. Sir William Swan, the King's Resident at Hamburgh, gave me an account of his sending my Books of the Garter to the Duke of Saxony, and Prince Elector of Brandenburgh, and gave me the said Prince his letter.[3]

Sept. 17. I waited on the King, and shewed him the gold chain the King of

---

[1] JOHN MAITLAND, 1616–82. Received title of Duke of Lauderdale in 1672.

[2] Sir JOHN DAVIS, matric. Gloucester Hall 1626, aged 15 ; knighted 1662.

[3] A. had received a letter from the Elector FRIEDRICH WILHELM, dated 24 March, 1674.

Denmark sent me, he liked it well, and gave me leave to wear it.[1]

[19.][2]

Oct. 2. 11.30 a.m. I and my wife first entered my house at South-Lambeth.

5. This night Mrs. Tredescant was in danger of being robbed, but most strangely prevented.

28. I waited on the Earl Marshal to gain his leave for disposing of my Herald's place. He told me I was a person of the ability, that he was loath to leave me, and put off the discourse to a further time.

Nov. 17. I received a case of excellent pistols, and a silver hilt for a sword, sent me as a present, from the Earl of Castlemaine,[3] from Liege.

26.[4] Mrs. Tredescant being willing to deliver up the Rarities to me, I carried several of them to my house.

---

[1] On the next day A. wrote to Count Griffinfield, Chancellor of Denmark, concerning the gold chain.—MS. *Ashmole*, 1131.

[2] Sept. 19. A. acknowledges receipt of one of Wood's books.—MS. *Wood* F, 39.

[3] ROGER PALMER, Earl Castlemaine 1634–1705, a mathematician. A. had a letter from him on Oct. 29 in return for one he wrote on the 21st.—MS. *Ashmole*, 1131.

[4] A. wrote a letter to Sir T. Browne on this date.—MS. *Ashmole*, 1131.

Dec. 1. I began to remove the rest of the Rarities to my house at South-Lambeth.

2. This night my affair about the enlarging my control upon the counties, was settled.

18. Mr. Lilly fell sick, and was let blood in the left foot, a little above the ankle, new moon the day before, and the sun eclipsed.

20. Mr. Lilly had a great pain in his left leg, which lasted 24 hours, and put him into a great fever.

23. My wife went to see him.

26. I went to visit him also.

28. The humour being fixed in two places upon the top of his left foot (one being the place he was let blood in) and now grown ripe, they were lanced by Mr. Agar, an Apothecary (and no less a good Chirurgeon) of Kingston, after which he began to be at more ease, and the fever abated.

I was present at this operation.

1675.

Jan. 6. I wore the chain of gold, sent me from the King of Denmark, before the King, in his proceeding to the chapel, to offer gold, frankincense, and myrrh.

20. The Earl of Winchelsea,[1] Sir William Swan, and Mr. Thynn,[2] were entertained at my Chamber in the Temple.

29. This afternoon I obtained the Earl Marshal's leave to resign my Herald's place.

Feb. 10. Colonel Gervais Hollis, a Master of the Requests, died.[3]

21. 2 p.m. I sealed the counterpart of Mr. Hopkin's mortgage of Little Pipe in Com. Stafford, to me for £400.

[23.][4]

25. Mr. Dethick[5] offered me £300, if I would resign my Herald's place to him.

Mar. 1. This night Mr. Sandford[6] offered me the like sum, if I would resign it to him.

9. Colonel Gervais Hollis's body (was) carried thro' London, toward Mansfield in Nottinghamshire, where he was buried.

---

[1] HENEAGE FINCH 2nd Earl Winchelsea, *d.* 1689 ; Ambassador at Constantinople 1661–9.

[2] THOMAS THYNNE the newly elected burgher for Oxford.

[3] JERVAIS HOLLIS " sergt.-major " ; secretary of petitions to Charles II. (D.N.B.)

[4] A. replied to queries about taxation of ecclesiastical benefices.—MS. *Wood* F, 39.

[5] GILBERT DETHICK matric. Ch. Ch. 1639, age 17. His father Henry was a son of Sir William Dethick, Garter and grandson of Sir Gilbert Dethick, Garter.

[6] FRANCIS SANDFORD, Lancaster herald 1676–89. (D.N.B.)

24. Lord Hatton and his sisters dined with me.

26. Mr. Smith of Moorfields died, he had an excellent good library of books.

April 17. My brother Dugdale having agreed with me for my Herald's place, I this morning moved the Earl Marshal that he might succeed me, which he granted.

The same morning I agreed with my carpenter for building the additional rooms I made to my house at South-Lambeth.

27. This afternoon Sir William Swan told me, the Prince Elector of Brandenburgh had given order for a present to me, and that it lay ready for me at Hamburgh.

May 1. 10.30 a.m. I and my wife came to my house at South-Lambeth, to lie there.

5. 10.20 a.m. I laid the first stone of my new buildings there.

20. This day Monsieur Swerene, the Prince Elector of Brandenburgh's Envoy came to visit me at my chamber in the Temple.

25. My wife in getting up of her horse near Farnham Castle, fell down, and hurt the hinder part of her head, and left shoulder.

June 6. Mr. Richard Hodgkinson (my old friend, and fellow Gentleman of the

Ordinance in the garrison of Oxford) was buried.

25. 6.30 a.m. The foundation of St. Paul's Church London, laid.

27. Dr. Barlow[1] (my old and worthy friend) consecrated Bishop of Lincoln.

July 15. This morning a Jury of Sewers set out my brick wall made toward the highway, at my house at South Lambeth.

21. 4 p.m. I surrendered my Herald's place to his Majesty in Chancery, before Sir —— Clerk, one of the Masters of that Court.

Aug. 28. 1.40 p.m. I and my wife came to dwell at my house at South Lambeth.

Oct. 7. Monsieur la Mere (lately sent from the Prince of Orange[2] to his Majesty) gave me a visit at my Chamber in the Temple.

8. I first became acquainted with Monsieur Spanheim,[3] the Prince Elector Palatine's Envoy to his Majesty ; 9.30 a.m. He was the Prince Elector Palatine's Plenipotentiary at Cologne, and there Sir Joseph Wil-

---

[1] Dr. THOMAS BARLOW matr. Queen's 1625 ; Bodley's librarian 1652–60 ; bishop of Lincoln 1675–†1691. (D.N.B.)

[2] PRINCE OF ORANGE *m.* Princess Mary 1677.

[3] EZEC. SPANHEIM, ambassador of King of Prussia, cre. D.C.L. 1706.

liamson delivered to him my Book of the Garter, to present to the said Prince.

26. My brother Dugdale created Windsor Herald.

27. Mr. Thomas Ross [1] (tutor to the Duke of Monmouth) died.

29. Between 9 and 10 p.m. my uncle Ralph Ashmole died.

Nov. 2. I fell ill of a cold.

7. Great pain in my farthest tooth, on the left side of my upper jaw, which continued three or four days.

16. 11 a.m. I began to plant my garden walls with fruit-trees.

This day Robert Chaloner, Lancaster Herald, died.

Dec. 4. I first became acquainted with Mr. Butler, Chaplain to the Duke of Ormond, and an able astrologian.

23. Between 10 and 11 a.m. Mr. Richard Sanders the astrologian died.

1676.

Feb. 27. Sir Thomas Chicheley,[2] and Sir Jonas Moore came to dine with me.

---

[1] THOMAS ROSS, keeper of King's libraries and groom of privy chamber, *d.* 1675.

[2] Sir THOMAS CHICHELEY 1618–94, Master-general of Ordnance ; M.P. Cambridge ; Knighted 1670.

Mar. 10. I fell ill of the toothache, and the farthest tooth in the upper side of my left jaw, was very loose.

29. My teeth fell looser, and put me to so great trouble, I could not chew my meat for a week.

31. My brother Harrison of Lichfield, died.

April 6. I was afflicted with the vertigo, and drew out my tooth that had so greatly troubled me.

7. The Officers of Arms seeming unwilling to let me have the Funeral-turn, which was my due, I acquainted the Earl Marshal with it, and this day, Sir Thomas St. George waiting on him, he told him, he would have me have the benefit of it. His Lordship afterward told me, that he said to Sir Thomas, " That he esteemed me the best " Officer in the Office, and if he could have " persuaded me to have stayed in the Office, " I should not have wanted the best employ- " ment, and have been made the fore-horse in " the team ; and that I had deserved greatly, " in getting money for re-building the " office."

April 16. This evening the gout took me in my left foot, and held me for a fortnight.

Aug. 8. I fell ill of a looseness, and had above twenty stools.

[*Sept.* 1.   Mrs. Tradescant signed her "Confession."] [1]

4.   Mr. Ogilby died. [2]

Nov. 20.   I fell ill of the gout in my left toe ; this fit held me a fortnight.

Dec. 18.   My old friend, Major Brookes, the stationer, died.

22. He was buried.

1677.

[Ashmole's notes on the weather, South Lambeth, start this year and continue to 1685.—MS. *Ashmole*, 438.]

Feb. 6.   My uncle Ralph Ashmole's widow died.

7. Afternoon I took cold in my head.

14. I took cold in my right ear.

19. Mr. Richard Edlin, [3] one of my clerks, died this night.

20. Sir Edward Walker, Garter, died suddenly.

21, 23, 25. I took *Pil: Macri* which did me much good.

21. Mr. Richard Edlin buried in St. Allhallows Churchyard.

---

[1] See p. 110, note.   [2] See p. 52, note.
[3] RICHARD EDLIN, 1631–77, author of *Observationes astrologicae* 1659 and *Prae-Nuncius Sydereus* 1664.

22. The Bishop of Salisbury [1] wrote to me, that he had moved the King to bestow Garter's place upon me. I wrote back to excuse my accepting of it, with desire to move no further on my behalf.

26. The Earl Marshal sent his Secretary, Mr. Hayes, to have my opinion, whether Garter's place was in the King's or his dispose. I gave my opinion, it was in the King's disposal.

Mar. 6. The Bishop of Salisbury came to my house, to acquaint me with the King's command, that I should assist him in making good the King's title to Garter's place.

28. 7 a.m. I laid the foundation of my back buildings to my house at South Lambeth.

30. The hearing before some of the Lords of the Council and some Knights of the Garter, between the King and Earl-Marshal, at which Garter's place was adjudged to be solely in the King's disposal.

31. Mr. Bartie earnestly pressed me to accept of Garter's place, intimating my Lord Treasurer thought me fittest for it, which I excused ; nevertheless he gave me an opportunity to speak with my Lord, which when

---

[1] SETH WARD, 1617–89, bishop of Salisbury 1667–89. A's reply to the letter is in his MS. 1134.

I had, I forebore saying any thing of this matter to him.

April 1. Mr. Bartie set more earnestly upon me to be Garter, but I absolutely refused.

2. My Father Dugdale was pitched upon to be Garter, and the King gave his consent ; whereupon the Earl Marshal sent for him out of Warwickshire by this night's post.

10. My Father Dugdale came to town.

11. The Earl Marshal told my Father Dugdale, that I had carried my self very fairly in the matter between the King and him, touching Garter's place.

[16. H. Coley sent A. an account of the motion of the great Comet. This and his own notes, dated 22nd April, are in MS. *Ashmole*, 242.]

May 10. 9 a.m. The first foundation of new building in Cheapside (was laid).

12. About noon I sprained my right foot, near my ankle.

24. My Father Dugdale created Garter, principal King of Arms.

25. He was knighted.

June 1. He took his oath in a chapter, called to that purpose.

7. My Lord Treasurer agreed to have my Comptrol continue upon the vouchers.

July 2. I sealed a lease of my house in Lichfield to Mr. Falkingham for eight years.

Another to Henry Aldridge of the lands in Hemewick, for seven years.

Another to Mr. William Webb, of the Moggs in Lichfield, for eleven years.

[Warrant for a fat buck from Windsor for Ashmole. MS. *Ashmole*, 1134.]

10. I made a feast at my house in South Lambeth, in honour of my benefactors to my work of the Garter.[1]

Aug. 1. I received £400 being the mortgage money I formerly lent upon Mr. Hopkin's estate, at little Pipe near Lichfield.

Sept. 10. 1 p.m. Mr. Rose, the King's gardener, died.[2]

17. Count Wallestein, Envoy Extraordinary from the Emperor, Marques d' Este Borgamainers, Envoy Extraordinary from the King of Spain, Monsieur Swerenc, Envoy Extraordinary from the Prince Elector of Brandenburgh, and the Count of Flamburgh bestowed a visit on me at my house at South Lambeth.

28. Fire in the Inner Temple.

---

[1] The names of both the dishes and guests at this feast are recorded in MS. *Ashmole*, 1134, but the object of the dinner is there stated as the dedication of his new dining-room.

[2] ROSE. See p. 82.

Oct. 4.　Mr. Loggan [1] began to draw my picture in black lead.

16. My Lord Bishop of Oxford [2] gave me a visit at Mr. Loggan's.

31. Myne Heere van Zeelim (Secretary to the Prince of Orange) came to visit me at my Chamber in the Temple. [3]

Nov. 4.　Mr. Rawlins, Town-Clerk of Lichfield, acquainted me, that Mr. Richard Dyott, [4] Parliament-man for that city, was likely to die, and that the Bailiffs, &c. were willing to choose me in his room ; but I answered, I had no inclination to accept of that honour, and therefore desired him to give my thanks to all that were so well affected to me.

10. Myne Heere van Zeelim, and the Dutch Ambassador's secretary came to my house to visit me.

Dec. 10.　Doctor Plot [5] came to me, to

---

[1] DAVID LOGGAN, "Chalcographus privilegiatus" 1672 ; began a portrait of Ashmole in 1677.

[2] Dr. JOHN FELL, 1625–86, dean of Christ Church, 1660–86; Bishop of Oxford, 1675–86.

[3] VAN ZELIM.

[4] Sir RICHARD DYOTT, s. of Anthony Dyott of Lichfield, see p. 49 ; B.A. from Corpus Christi Coll. 1607 ; *d.* 1659.

[5] DR. ROBERT PLOT, 1640–96, the celebrated author of *The Natural History of Oxfordshire* ; first keeper of the Ashmolean Museum 1683.

See Evelyn's letter in Appendix, p. 169.

request me to nominate him to be Reader at
Oxford, of the Philosophical Lecture upon
natural things.   I told him if the University
liked of him, he should have my suffrage.

[12. A. wrote to Sir Sam. Morland about
the representation of Lichfield.] [1]

19. 2 p.m.   Mrs. Ogilby [2] died.

This morning my tooth, next my fore-
tooth, in my upper jaw, was very loose, and
I easily pulled it out.

Having received several letters from Lichfield, to request me to stand for a Parliament-
man there, I at length consented, provided
it was not too late ; and upon attempting it
by others for me, found it was so ; for I
found the magistrates and friends not so
cordial to me as I expected, and therefore
I drew off and would not stand. [3]

1678.

Feb. 9.   One of my middle teeth, in my
lower jaw, was broke out while at dinner.

[1] MS. *Ashmole*, 1731.
[2] Probably widow of JOHN OGILBY, see pp. 52 and 104.
[3] Many of these letters are preserved. A. wrote to Sir H.
Archbold, J. Dugdale (12 letters), Magistrates of Lichfield,
J. Rawlins, M. Smalewood Dean of Lichfield, J. Stubbes
(see MS. *Ashmole*, 1731), and to Sir Leoline Jenkins (MS.
Ashmole, 1131).

March 23. The gout took me in my right toe.

April 4. 11.30 a.m. My wife told me, Mrs. Tredescant[1] was found drowned in her pond. She was drowned the day before about noon, as appeared by some circumstances.

6. 8 p.m. She was buried in a vault in Lambeth Churchyard, where her husband and his son John had been formerly laid.

22. I removed the pictures from Mrs. Tredescant's house to mine.

May 11. My Lord Bishop of Oxford and Dr. Nicholas,[2] Vice-Chancellor of Oxford, gave me a visit at my house, 7.30 a.m.

June 18. Mr. Lea and his wife's release to me of the £100 I was to pay after Mrs. Tredescant's death, bears date.

July 17. About 8 a'clock this morning I was served with a subpœna, out of the Chancery, at Mr. Searle's suit.

Aug. 5. The Earl of Peterborough came to visit me at my Chamber in the Temple, and to see my collection of coins.

---

[1] ESTER TRADESCANT appears to have been greatly worried by A's living next door. Her tragic " confession " is printed in Gunther's *Early Science in Oxford*, vol. iii, p. 290.

[2] Dr. JOHN NICHOLAS, D.D., warden of New college, 1675–9.

Sept. 28. I took my purging pills.
29. I bled with leeches.

1679.

Jan. 26. 10 p.m. The fire at the Temple began next room to my Chamber, and burned my library, &c.

Mar. 25. I entered upon the house and ground adjoining to my house in South Lambeth, which Mr. Bartholomew let me a lease of.

31. 9.45 a.m. Mr. Bartholomew sealed my lease.

April. I became first acquainted with my Lord Roberts.

June 8. I went toward Great Linford in Buckinghamshire, to Sir —— Napier,[1] and came thither next day, 8 p.m.

14. I returned to London.

27. I visited Monsieur Spanheim.

[*July* 23.][2]

---

[1] ? Sir RICHARD NAPIER, fellow of All Souls 1628 ; M.D. 1642 ; F.R.S.

[2] 23 July. "Went to see Mr. Ashmole's Library and curiosities at Lambeth. He has divers MSS. but most of them astrological, to which study he is addicted, though I believe not learned, but very industrious, as his *History of the Order of the Garter* proves. He showed me a toad included in amber. The prospect from a turret is very fine, it being so near London, and yet not discovering any house about the country." Evelyn, *Diary.*

Aug. 15. My Lord Grace of Canterbury, (Dr. Sancroft)[1] came to visit me at my house, and spent a great part of the day with me in my study.

25. Sir Jonas Moore, Surveyor of the Ordnance, and my old friend, died.

Sept. 2. Sir Jonas Moore buried in the Tower-Church.

About the end of October I was much troubled with the vertigo.

1680.

Mar. 15. 8 p.m. I fell ill of the gout in my left great toe.

20. It fell into my right great toe. This fit held me five weeks.

April 17. My wife fell ill of a rheumatism.

June 28. The Countess of Clarendon[2] came to visit me and my wife.

July 26. The Archbishop of Canterbury's sister and niece came to visit my wife.

Sept. 6. The Earl of Radnor,[3] Lord

---

[1] Dr. WILLIAM SANCROFT, archbishop of Canterbury 1678–90.

[2] See page 87, note.

[3] Sir JOHN ROBARTES, cre. 1st Earl of Radnor 1679.

President of the Council, with his lady and daughters, dined at my house.

15. 5.30 p.m. Sir Charles Cotterell presented me to the Prince Elector Palatine, in the Council-Chamber, whose hand I kissed, and had much discourse with him about the Order of the Garter, into which he was ready to be elected.

16. 2 p.m. I presented the said Prince with one of my Books of the Garter ; which he courteously received, and now I had much more discourse with him.

18. Sir Charles Cotterell told me this morning, that one of the Prince Elector's Gentlemen came to him the day before, to desire me to dine with him this day. Hereupon I attended him accordingly, and he placed me next himself, on his left hand, and received me with great respect ; and when he rose, took me aside, and told me he had heard much of my worth and esteem, and desired to have correspondency with me, after he returned into his country, &c.

Sept. 24. This day between 11 and 12, my esteemed good friend Mr. John Staniesby of Clements-Inn died : he fell sick at Northampton the 17th instant between 11 and 12 a'clock, as he was coming toward London, from his native country, Derbyshire. He was buried the 26th of September at night, in a vault, in St. Clements Danes Church, under the seats belonging to the gentlemen of Clements-Inn. He gave me this legacy by his will, *viz. ITEM, I give to my honoured Friend Elias Ashmole, Esq; and his Wife, each of them a Ring of Twenty Shillings value, and likewise what Books in my Study he shall please to make choice of (many of them being his noble Gift to me after I had lost many of my own by the Fire at my Chamber).*

The Prince Elector Palatine, at his departure, 18 September, put a medal of gold into Sir Charles Cotterell's hands, which had his father's picture on the one side, and an escutcheon of his arms on the other, supported by a lion; and bade him to deliver it to me, and to assure me, that, when he came home, he would also send me one of his own, it weighs . . .

27. This day, Sir Charles Cotterell sent me the medal.

Nov. 4. 12.30 p.m. Mr. Bartholomew sealed me a new lease of my house, &c. in South Lambeth.

16. I received from the hands of Sir

Robert Southwell,[1] lately return'd from Berlin, a gold chain with a medal, from the Elector of Brandenburgh : It is composed of 90 links of philagreen links in great knobs, most curious work. Upon the one side is the Elector's effigie, on the other, the view of Strallsund, and made upon the rendition of that city into his hands. It weighs 22 ounces.

29. I waited on the King, and acquainted him with the honour the Elector of Brandenburg had done me, and shewed him the chain. He liked it well and commended the workmanship.

[*Dec.* 1. This day A. wrote to Baron Schwerin, the Elector of Brandenburg's minister. Also to R. Rockwood, but the letter was not sent owing to R's reported death. Also to Charles Bertie, envoy of the Elector Palatine. MS. *Ashmole*, 1131.]

1681.

Feb. 9. Mr. William Chiffinch, Closet-Keeper to the King, dined at my house, and then told me his nephew, Thomas

---

[1] Sir ROBERT SOUTHWELL matr. Queens 1653 ; clerk of privy council 1664 ; envoy extraordinary to Elector of Brandenburg ; president of Royal Society (5 times) ; *d.* 1702.

Chiffinch (son to Thomas Chiffinch, my most worthy friend) died the week before.

March 15. Between 9 and 10 a.m. Mr. Butler, the minister and astrologian, brought me acquainted with Sir Edward Deering, brother to Sir Edward Deering, now one of the Lords Commissioners of the Treasury.

April 5. Having been very lame in the hollow of my right foot most part of the winter (occasioned, as I suppose, by applying poultices to my gout, which relaxed my tendons) this evening my pains were so increased I could scarce go, and put me into so great a heat, that I became very feverish, and my urine pricked me sore as it came from me.

6. I took my usual sweat, which made me well, and strengthened my tendons, so that the next day I went to London, and walked much up and down the streets, without any pain, at night I became hot, and slept ill.

9. 11.45 p.m. I fell into a cold fit of an ague, which, with the hot fit, held me seven hours.

11. I took early in the morning, good dose of elixir, and hung three spiders about my neck, and they drove my ague away ——*Deo gratias*.

14. Dr. Gunning, Bishop of Ely,[1] came this afternoon to visit me at my house, and stayed in my study till night.

May 19. My worthy friend and neighbour, both at the Temple, and in the country, Thomas Siderfin, Esq., died, near Epsom, about 4 p.m.

24. Mr. Siderfin was buried in Lambeth Church.

25. At the end of dinner Mr. Lilly's left side of his mouth was drawn aside, but recovered again.

30. This evening the dead palsy seized on the left side of my old friend, Mr. William Lilly, astrologer.

June 2. Mr. Lilly took a vomit, at night he took his bed.

4. I went to visit him, but found him beyond hope.

9. 3 a.m. Mr. Lilly died.

10. 8 p.m. He was buried in the Chancel of Walton Church.

12. I bought Mr. Lilly's library of books of his widow for £50.

17. I sold one of my Chambers at the Temple to Mr. —— Holt, for £138, and this evening he was admitted.

---

[1] Dr. PETER GUNNING, master of Corpus Christi college 1660 ; Bishop of Ely 1675-84.

This day my god-daughter —— the only child of my neighbour, Thomas Siderfin, Esq., died.

July 1. Mr. Sawbridge the stationer, an old friend of Mr. Lilly's and mine, died.

6. Mr. Sawbridge buried in the middle aisle of St. Brides Church Fleet-Street.

This day my wife went toward Blyth-Hall, with Sir William Dugdale, her father, to visit her mother.

Aug. 12. Sir George Wharton[1] died at Enfield between one and two in the morning.

18. My wife returned from Blyth-Hall.

25. Sir George Wharton buried in the Tower.

Sept. 19. My wife miscarried, having gone about 3 months.

Oct. 1. I took purging physic.

2. I took my sweat for prevention of the gout.

4. About 8 a.m. I fell sick of the colic, which held me with sharp pains, especially on my right side, for 24 hours : and then I was presently eased, by applying bay-salt and bran, heated in a frying-pan ; but before nothing else could ease me.

---

[1] Sir GEORGE WHARTON, astrologer, created baronet 1677.

24. Mr. Thomas Flatman[1] came to my house to visit me.

Nov. 1. Mrs. Lilly came to my house, and stayed a week.

4. About 9 a.m. I sealed an assignment of my judgment of £1200 formerly given me by Sir Robert Thomas, and about an hour after, received from Sir Robert Clayton[2] £800 a composition agreed on with Sir Robert Thomas, out of which I gave him £70.

Dec. 18.[3] About 4 p.m. my dear mother-in-law, the Lady Dugdale, died.

21. She was buried in a sepulchre made in the chancel of Shustock Church, by Sir William Dugdale, for himself and her.

1682.

Mar. 10. About 5 p.m. I received a summons, to appear at a Lodge to be held the next day at Masons' Hall London.

11. Accordingly I went, and about noon

---

[1] THOMAS FLATMAN matr. New coll. 1655 ; F.R.S. 1668 ; " eminent poet " ; *d.* 1688.

[2] Sir ROBERT CLAYTON ? knighted 1671 ; Lord Mayor of London 1679–80.

[3] Vide last page of Sir W. Dugdale's Life—Lond. 1714. 8vo.

were admitted into the Fellowship of Free-Masons, Sir William Wilson,[1] Knight, Captain Richard Borthwick, Mr. William Woodman, Mr. William Grey, Mr. Samuel Taylour, and Mr. William Wise.

I was the Senior Fellow among them (it being 35 years since I was admitted) ; there were present besides my self the Fellows after named, Mr. Thomas Wise, Master of the Masons Company this present year ; Mr. Thomas Shorthose, Mr. Thomas Shadbolt, —— Waindsford, Esq. ; Mr. Nicholas Young, Mr. John Shorthose, Mr. William Hamon, Mr. John Thompson, and Mr. William Stanton. We all dined at the *Half-Moon-Tavern* in Cheapside, at a noble dinner prepared at the charge of the new accepted Masons.

April 1. My wife fell ill of a rheumatism ; it began in her left ankle, then into her left knee and right toe.

18. Sir Charles Cotterell carried me to the Morocco Ambassador.

Alcade Abdelloe, and Bomonzore came to my house, and dined with me.

---

[1] Sir WILLIAM WILSON, architect and builder, knighted in 1681, who had carved a statue of Charles II for west front of Lichfield cathedral. He built Nottingham Castle and *d.* 1710, aged 70.

May 17.   George Smaldridge was elected out of Westminster-School to go to Christ-Church in Oxford.[1]

20. The Marquis of Worcester and Earl of Aylesbury, with their eldest sons, gave me a visit at my house this afternoon.

22. This night, scratching the right side of my buttock, above the fundament, thence proceeded a violent sharp humour.

25. I applied poultices thereto (and now was not able to sit or lie upon my bed); it was made of white bread-crumbs, oil of roses and rose-leaves.

28. The poultice having well drawn the humour out, I applied *Unguentum Nutritum* to it.

June 4.   Being hard bound in my body I was five hours before I could go to stool, and suffered much torment.

9. I purged with pills.

13. I went abroad again, thanks be to God.

17. Bomansur dined with me, and gave me several excellent receipts.

---

[1] GEORGE SMALRIDGE, s. of Thomas S. of Lichfield ; matric. Ch. Ch. 1682, aged 18 ; bishop of Bristol 1714 ; *d.* 1719, aged 57. His fees at Westminster school were paid by Ashmole, whose life he contemplated writing.

[*July* 3.] [1]

5. The Morocco Ambassador dined at my house.

13. The Astrologers' Feast restored by Mr. Moxon.[2]

16. The Lord Lansdowne,[3] and Sir William Haward gave me a kind visit at my house.

20. The Morocco Ambassador made ready to go away, but the Alcade slipped out of his lodgings, and hindered his journey.

21. The Alcade was taken.

22. This morning I gave the Morocco Ambassador a large magnifying glass.[4] In the afternoon the Alcade returned to the Ambassador's lodgings.

---

[1] On 3 July 1682 A. wrote to Wood, " I am sorry I cannot at present give you any account of Mr. William Cole. But as he, so some others (that have dedicated Bookes to me) were indeed strangers to me, and I never heard of them after. Beside the stationer is dead, and there I am at a loss also. But I will not rest here, but beare it in mind. . . ." MS. *Wood* F. 39.

[2] JOSEPH MOXON, 1627–1700, hydrographer and mathematician.

[3] GEORGE GRANVILLE 1667–1735. Lord Lansdown.

[4] Under date 1681–2 11 June, Evelyn noted that the Moroccan Ambassador named Hamet was entertained on May 30 at Oxford, " and about the same time dined with Elias Ashmole, who made him a present of a magnifying glass." *Diary*.

23. About 3 in the morning the Ambassador went away.

Aug. 16. I went toward Oxford, to see the building prepared to receive my rarities where I arrived about 7 a'clock in the evening.

17. Between 8 and 9. I first saw the said building. I was invited by the Vice-Chancellor, and dined with him at Queen's-College.[1]

22. 6.30 p.m. I arrived back at my house.

Oct. 23. My Lord Chancellor Finch[2] sent for me to cure him of his rheumatism. I dined there, but would not undertake the cure.

1683.

Jan. 23. I took a great cold, going by water, and kept my chamber three days.

29. The Astrologers' Feast held at the *Three Cranes* in Chancery-Lane, Sir Edward Deering and the Town-Clerk of London stewards.

---

[1] TIMOTHY HALTON, provost of Queen's College.
[2] Sir HENEAGE FINCH, matric. Ch. Ch. 1635 aged 14 ; Lord Chancellor 1675 ; *d.* 1682. (D.N.B.)

Feb. 2. My picture (after sent to Oxford) came home 3 p.m. I acquainted Mr. Woolrich,[1] in part, with the secret of raising flowers from a virgin-earth.

15. I began to put up my Rarities into cases to send to Oxford.[2]

Mar. 7. I took purging pills, which wrought very well.

10. The gout fell into my left great toe this morning.

14. The last load of my Rarities sent to the barge. This afternoon I relapsed into the gout.

21. The gout fell into my right great toe.

April 8. Major Huntingdon came to my house, to visit me.

10. I took my pills, and purged very well.

11. The pains in my feet returned.

24. Mr. Anthony Bowyer, and his lady, came to visit me and my wife.

25. I went first abroad, after so long confinement by reason of my gout.

---

[1] JOHN WOOLRIDGE, agricultural author, 1669.

[2] Ashmole's Rarities included the scientific collections of the two Tradescants. They were exhibited in the Ashmolean Museum until 1860, when they were removed to the new Science Museum in the Parks. In 1926 a few of the original specimens were again brought back to the Old Ashmolean, the building which had been specially built by the University for their reception in 1683.

ASHMOLEAN MUSEUM.

From a Drawing in the possession of Thos. Dunbar Esqr.

THE ASHMOLEAN MUSEUM

26. Dr. Smallwood, Dean of Lichfield, died.[1]

[*May* 21. Museum opened.][2]

Aug. 6. The Surveyors of the High-ways began to raise the causeway at Horshead-Still.

9. They finished their work, all at my charge.

Sept. 5. I took pills.

6. I took a sweat.

7. I took leeches, all wrought very well.

17. Monsieur Job Ludolph [3] [that wrote the *Historia Æthiopiae*] came to visit me [at South Lambeth].

23. I first saw Dr. Lister,[4] at my Lord Archbishop of Canterbury's at dinner.

---

[1] MATHEW SMALWOOD matr. B.N.C. 1632, aged 18 ; D.D. 1660 ; chaplain to Charles II ; dean of Lichfield 1671 ; *d.* 1683.

[2] On this day Ashmole's Museum was opened by the Duke of York. The circumstances are narrated in Gunther's *Early Science in Oxford*, iii, pp. 306–317, where the letter of thanks from the University and Ashmole's *Rules* for his museum are printed. Charles II's monogram C.II. is carved over the Broad Street entrance to the building. It may have been due to the Rye House Plot of a few days before, that the King himself did not perform the opening ceremony, but deputed his brother, the Duke of York, to do it for him.

[3] JOB LUDOLPHUS attended meetings of the Royal Society. Spratt *History R.S.* iv, p. 218, 254. Two letters from him to A. dated Paris, Dec. 1683 are extant. MS. *Ashmole*, 1136.

[4] MARTIN LISTER, M.D. Oxon by diploma 1683–4, *Munk's Roll.*

24. The Prince Elector of the Rhine his Secretary dined with me, so also a nobleman of that country, a son of a Patrician of Nuremberg, and Dr. Lister.[1]

26. A stitch took me at the setting on of my left hip.

28. I was very much troubled with it.

Oct. 8. Monsieur Ludolph, and his son, dined with me.

10. I gave Mr. Heyseg[2] a Book of the Garter, my wife gave him three gold buckles.

16. The Commissioners of the Excise dined with me.

30. I took leave with Monsieur Job Ludolph, and his son, who were returning into Germany.

Nov. Monsieur Ludolph went from London.

---

[1] The names of A's guests are given in his note on MS. 1136 f 102. "CHRISTOPHORUS FURER, son to Johes Christophorus Furer; one of the Septemvirs of Norimberg and one of the four praefecti militiae of that Republique." "FRITZ DIETRICH SPIEGEL VON PICKELSHEIM, a Palatine gent. and Mr. DAVID RIESMAN, private secretary to the Prince Elector Palatine all three gave me a visit the 24 Sept. 1683, and dyned with me at S. Lambeth."

[2] Mr. JOHN HEYSIG, a Swedish author, who was proposed as a candidate for the Royal Society. Cf. Spratt *History R.S.* iv, p. 111. He presented a runic calendar to the Ashmolean Museum in 1683.

Dec. 7.   A boil began under my chin.

26. 6.30 a.m.   I had a long fit of a vertigo.

1684.

Feb. 4.   Mr. Jean Schielderrey, the Bishop of Bergen's son, and Mr. Godfreed Ross, a Prussian, visited me, [being recommended by Dr. Plot].

Mar. 5. 11 a.m.   A green staff was sent me by the Steward of St. Thomas's Hospital, with signification that I was chosen one of the Governors.

April 6.   Major Huntingdon dined with me.

8. The Installation of Prince of Denmark.[1]

21. Major Huntingdon died, and this day Mr. Thomas Henshaw, Dr. Rogers, Dr. More, and Dr. Bernard[2] dined at my house.

30. Major Huntingdon was buried at St. Botolph's Aldersgate.

May 5. 2 p.m.   I laid the foundation of my new stable.

14. I took a sweat.

---

[1] GEORGE PRINCE OF DENMARK, *m.* Princess Anne 1683.

[2] ? Dr. EDWARD BERNARD, 1638–96, Savilian professor of astronomy 1673–91 ; rector of Brightwell, Berks.

19. Sir Thomas Walcot [1] came to visit me.

June 27. I bruised my left great toe.

July 18. 10.15 a.m. My two coach-horses were brought home.

22. My coach brought home.

23. I went toward Oxford.

[27.] [2]

28. I returned home.

Aug. 4. Several French gentlemen, and Johannes Serenius Chodowieskey, a Polander, came to visit me [at South Lambeth (he) promised to give me some account of Albert de Lascky, the Polish Count Palatine, with whom Dr. Dee went into Germany].

6. I rubbed the skin near my rump, whereupon it began to be very sore.

8. I purged.

9. I took leeches.

10. I purged again.

12. I applied a plaster to it.

15. Mr. Agar applied a balsam.

17. The sore began to break.

18. Dr. Plot, sent from Oxford to visit me, came to me. [3]

[1] Sir T. WALCOT.

[2] 27 July 1684. " Good sr. I should have been very glad to have found you in Towne, while I staid there ; that I might have kist your hand and delivered the enclosed myself." *Letter* of A. to Wood. MS. *Wood* F, 39.

[3] Doubtless to receive the Ashmolean Statutes.

19. I fell into a looseness, which continued for two days.

24. Mr. Agar lanced the sore.

26. Being hard bound, I was two hours before I could go to stool, and then with exceeding trouble.

31. I was again lanced, to prevent a fistula.

Sept. 10. By this time the sore, near my fundament, was healed.

Oct. 20. Sir Thomas Duppa,[1] and Mr. Mathews dined with me.

Nov. 19. Dr. Plot presented me with his Book, *de Origine Fontium*, which he had dedicated to me.

24. My teeth began to be loose.

[*Dec.* 5. A. wrote to Bp. Mew, the new bishop of Winchester. MS. *Ashmole*, 1136.]

8. Mr. Haack[2] brought Mr. Bowen of Upton in Pembrokeshire, to visit me.

19. Dr. Chamberlain proposed to me to bring Dr. Lister to my wife, that he might undertake her.

22. They both came to my house, and Dr. Lister did undertake her.

---

[1] Sir THOMAS DUPPA, made Black Rod and knighted 6 May, 1683.

[2] THEODORE HAAK 1605–90, original fellow of Royal Society.

1685.

Jan. 24. I was much troubled with my teeth, in my upper jaw, on my left side, which, by fits, continued for a week ; and then I held pills in my mouth, made of burnt alum, pepper, and tobacco, which drew much rheum from me, and so I was eased.

Feb. 6. King Charles II, my gracious master, died.

14. About 9 p.m. he was buried.

13. I took a violent cold, which held me till the 5th of the next month.

26. I took my purging pills.

27. I took my sweat, both worked exceeding well.

[27.] [1]

Mar. 2. 5.15 p.m. I received an obliging

---

[1] Under date " S. Lambeth 27 Feb. 1684/5," Ashmole wrote to Wood concerning Dee.

" I here furnish you with some materialls relating to Dr. Arthur Dee in two letters sent me from Dr. Tho. Browne of Norwich and one from my brother-in-law Mr. Henry Newcome at Manchester, to whom I wrote to gather what information he could relating to Dr. John Dee (sometyme Warden of that Colledge) his Father.

" When I had almost printed off my *Translation of Fasciculus Chemicus* (wch in 1650 I published, under the borrowed name of *James Hassolle*) I heard that Dr. Arthur Dee, the Author, was alive and dwelt at Norwich (though long before my inquiry as to that point became fruitless) I thereupon

letter from the Bailiffs, Justices, &c. of
Lichfield ; so also from the Dean,[1] inviting
me to stand to be one of their Burgesses for
Parliament.   I sent them word that I would
stand.

3. Whereupon they set about getting
votes for me,[2] and I found the citizens very
affectionate and hearty.

24. About a fortnight after my Lord
Dartmouth [3] told me, the King would take
it kindly from me, if I would give way
to Mr. Lewson.

25. 6.15 p.m.   Upon this I applied my
self to my Lord Treasurer, and desired him

dispatcht a Post letter thither, acquainting him what I had
done. E. ASHMOLE."

With this letter is also an extract from the letter of Sir T.
Browne, dated 25 Jan. 1658.—MS. *Ballard* 14, ff. 13, 14.

A second letter on Arthur Dee bearing date 28 March
1685 is in MS. *Wood* F, 39.

---

[1] DEAN ADDISON.

[2] FLOYER wrote to A., " we have twice asked votes for you
from house to house " 9 May 1685. MS. *Rawlinson*, D 864.
Seven letters are extant from A. to Symon Marten of
Lichfield relating to his candidature for parliament. They
bear dates from March 17 to May 5 1685. A's withdrawal
at the King's request is dated April 2 1687.—MS. *Rawlinson*,
D 864.

[3] GEORGE LEGGE, 1648–91, Lord Dartmouth ; Master-
General of Ordnance 1682.

to know the King's pleasure, by whom I found it was the King's desire, and then I immediately wrote down, to acquaint my friends that I would resign.

31. 5 p.m. But they would not believe my letter, which occasioned me to go to the King, and let him know so much, who told me he did not know I stood, when he gave Mr. Lewson encouragement to go down, for if he had, he would not have done it ; I told him I was all obedience, which he took very kindly. I then wrote down again, to assure them I would sit down, and so Mr. Lewson, with the assistance of my votes, carried it at the day of election.

April 1. 6 p.m. I first became acquainted with Mr. Negos, Secretary to the Duke of Norfolk.

27. Mr. ——[1] of Nuremberg, and a French gentleman, which Mr. Labadie[2] brought along with him, dined with me.

May 1. Judge Walcot, and Mr. Cook, the prothonotary dined with me.

4. Monsieur Spanheim, Envoy Extra-

---

[1] Possibly J. W. IM HOFF, see p. 142, but more probably Mr. Furer, see p. 126, note.

[2] ? JACQUES ABBADIE, 1654?–1727, D.D., Minister of French Church at Berlin, appointed by Fred. William ; elector of Brandenburg, *c.* 1680.

ordinary from the Elector of Brandenburgh, and his lady, Monsieur Bessor,
his agent here, with Sir Charles Cotterell, his son and his lady, dined with
me.

5. The Duke of Norfolk [1] invited me to
dine with him the next day, which I did,
and was well received.

13. I took my purging pills.

14. And my sweat.

29. I visited Dr. Smith, Bishop of Carlisle,
who was of my ancient acquaintance at
Oxford.

31. This night a pain (in my sleep)
took me in my middle toe of my right foot,
which removed to my ankle, and after three
days went away.

June 2. A pain took the furthermost
tooth but one, on the right side of my upper-
most jaw.

4. My said tooth sunk so low I could not
chew.

9. A boil rose in the left side of my
throat.

17. This evening I had a grievous fit of
tooth-ache.

[1] HENRY HOWARD 6th Duke of Norfolk 1677–84. Presented his Library to the Royal Society and Arundel Marbles
to Oxford.

July 9.[1] The Countess of Clarendon,[2] Bishop of St. Asaph,[3] Mr. Henshaw,[4] Mr. Evelyn,[5] Dr. Tenison,[6] and Mr. Frasier supped at my house.

11. Earl of Radnor[7] fell sick about noon.

17. 1 p.m. The Earl of Radnor died.

20. Dr. Ridgley (my old acquaintance) gave me a visit.

21. I went to Windsor, to the Installation of the Duke of Norfolk, Earl of Peterborough, and Lord Treasurer.

25. Earl of Radnor's body carried into Cornwall.

Aug. 4. I and my wife went to Mr. Napier's at Brockhill.

[1] July 9. "I supped this night at Lambeth at my old friend's Mr. Elias Ashmole's, with my Lady Clarendon, the Bishop of St. Asaph and Dr. Tenison, when we were treated at a great feast." Evelyn *Diary.*
On June 14, 1680, the Countess of Clarendon, Dr. Lloyd Dean of Bangor (since Bishop of St. Asaph) and Mr. Henshaw dined with Evelyn.

[2] FLOWER, COUNTESS OF CLARENDON, see page 87, note.

[3] WILLIAM LLOYD, 1627–1717 ; bishop of St. Asaph 1680–92.

[4] TH. HENSHAW see p. 62.

[5] JOHN EVELYN, 1620–1706, Secretary of the Royal Society 1672.

[6] TH. TENISON, bishop of Lincoln 1691–4 ; archbishop 1694.

[7] Sir JOHN ROBARTES, 1606–85, created Earl of Radnor 1679.

5. We went to Mr. Hutchinson's at Delroe.

8. We returned home.

10. A boil began to appear in my right groin.

13. This night my boil broke.

15. Another appeared a little higher, but it died.

24. I went to Windsor, to the Installation of the Earl of Feversham.[1]

Sept. 5. Passing upon the Thames, I took a great cold.

9. I took a purge.

10. I took a sweat.

Oct. 13. I took my sweat.

28. The Earl of Peterborough showed me his rare collection of gems and ancient rings.

30. I became acquainted with Mr. Cary, who lately came from Berlin, he told me his Electoral Highness of Brandenburg did often speak with a great deal of honour of me, and designed to have my Book of the Garter translated into Dutch.

Nov. 10. This morning I had some discourse with Mr. Gerard, about purchasing Mr. Plommer's farm.

---

[1] Sir GEORGE SONDES, created Earl of Feversham 1676 *d.* 1677.

16. Mr. Dean of Windsor, and Dr. Chamberlain the civilian, brought Sir John Faulconer of Scotland, to dine with me ; I found him a very ingenious gentleman, well read in his own country antiquities and coins.

Dec. 3. I first sat upon the Commissioners of Sewers, it being opened this morning, and my self named therein ; but nothing further was done at this sitting.

14. Sir John Faulconer dined with me, and I gave him divers of my English coins.

16. I waited on the Earl of Clarendon,[1] Lord Lieutenant of Ireland, as far as St. Albans in his journey thither. The jolting of the coach, which drove very hard, raised a swelling in my left breech.

1686.

Jan. 9. Mr. Cook, my neighbour at South-Lambeth, having lately set up a pale along his garden, and encroached upon the Church-Way about two foot, I undertook to complain of it, and this day Mr. Cooper, his landlord, and my self, upon

---

[1] HENRY HYDE, 1638–1709, friend of Evelyn, Earl of Clarendon, husband of Flower, widow of Sir Wm. Backhouse of Swallowfield, †22 Aug. 1669. Succeeded to the title 1674.

debate of the matter agreed (by his consent)
to set it back a foot and a half, which was
done accordingly.

[16.] [1]

20. The Commissioners of Sewers met,
and I (with some other of the Commissioners) took my oath.

Feb. 1. Sir John Faulconer,[2] a Scotch
gentleman, died.

4. He was buried this night at St.
Margaret's, Westminster.

10. This morning I dreamed, that being
at my old house in Sheere-Lane, the side of
the garret seemed to totter and fall, insomuch
that I thought the house it self would presently fall down.

This afternoon, about one a'clock, Sir
William Dugdale, my wife's father, died.

14. I moved the Duke of Norfolk, on my
brother Dugdale's behalf, that he would
move the King, that he might succeed him,
which he promised to do, (but I found him
more inclinable to prefer Sir Thomas St.
George). In his discourse he told me, no
man was fitter for the place than my self,
if I would accept of it ; but I made the

---

[1] 16 Jan. 1686. A. wrote a long letter to Wood on Sir
John Davis and Forman.—MS. *Wood* F, 39.

[2] Sir J. FAULCONER.

same excuse to him, as I did to his father, after the death of Sir Edward Walker.

19. The Duke of Norfolk proposed to me, to give my brother Dugdale the place of Norroy, and the next day gave him assurance of it.

Mar. 26. This night I pist so much, that I feared a diabetes, notwithstanding I had kept my self very temperate all the springtime.

27. This morning I grew ill and very hot, and was troubled with sharpness of urine. I took syrup of white lilies in posset-drink, and the next day an emulsion of the four cooling seeds, (this kept me temperate) with water of violets and wood-bine, to wash my mouth, and giving my self rest and ease, I thank God, I recovered in a few days.

April 5. I took my sweat.

May 6. My wife took Dr. Nagel's tincture.

17. I first dined at St. Thomas's Hospital, the general Court being held there this day.

20. 11.15 a.m. I first sat upon the Commission for Charitable Uses.

23. Dr. Plot presented me with his *Natural History of Staffordshire.*

[25.] [1]

26. Mr. Plummer sealed his part of the conveyance of his farm to me, and his wife acknowledged a fine before the Chief Justice of the Common Pleas.

[*June* 21.   Final draft of Statutes.]

July 10.   This morning early the fang-tooth in the right side of my upper jaw fell out.

13.   I began to repair my barn at South-Lambeth for Goodman Ingram.

25.   I took my sweat.

Aug. 2.   I and my wife went to Brockhill to Mr. Napier's.

7.   We went to Delroe to Mr. Hutchinson's.

9.   We returned to South-Lambeth.

13.   The gout fell into my left great toe : I applied leeches.

20.   The gout fell into my right great toe, I applied leeches.

28.   I applied black snails to my right foot, they being bruised ; but they blistered and poisoned the top of my foot, and after several breakings out, it was healed toward the middle of October.

Sept. 8.   I took my usual sweat.

---

[1] 25 May 1686.   A. wrote a letter on Sir Wm. Dugdale. —MS. *Wood* F, 39.

23. 5.30 p.m. I agreed upon conditions with Goodman Ingram, to make him a lease of the farm I bought of Mr. Plummer, except the oat-field.[1]

29. Sir Philip Floyd (who had the reversion of my office in the Excise) died.

Oct. 7. I waited on the King, upon his return to town from Windsor, who was pleased to receive me with much kindness.

12. I took a great cold in my neck, which held me six days.

25. 6.45 p.m. I sealed the lease to John Ingram.

26. The running gout seized on my wife's right instep. It continued shifting into her arms and knees with great torment till after Easter, and then she began to set her feet on the ground, yet (was) not able to go abroad till toward midsummer.

29. I received a letter from Sir (Henry) Chauncey,[2] Treasurer of the Temple, to invite me to the Bench, but I wrote him an excuse ; and next day gave him reasons for my refusal.

Dec. 7. The Commissioners of Excise

[1] Plommer's Farm, purchased by A. of John Plommer gent. and bequeathed to his wife.

[2] Sir HENRY CHAUNCY, 1632–1719. Topographer ; knighted 1681. A's letter to him is in MS. *Ashmole*, 1136.

moved the Lord Treasurer, showing the necessity of my having another clerk, and obtained £80 per annum salary for him.

23. 10.30 a.m. I received my order from the Lord Treasurer, for a new clerk, with £80 per annum salary.

This day my nephew Dugdale (Sir John Dugdale's son) was married.

1687.

Jan. 5. Earl of Rochester [1] surrendered his staff.

6. About 6 p.m. The Commission for the Lords Commissioners of the Treasury was opened and read.

8. This morning the Commissioners of the Excise, and my self, waited on the new Lords Commissioners of the Treasury.

13. The gout fell into my right hand, which disabled me from using my pen for above a quarter of a year.

16. I took my sweat.

17, 18, 19. I was much troubled with the wind-colic.

24. I applied leeches to my right hand.

27. The swelling of my hand abated.

---

[1] LAURENCE HYDE, Earl of Rochester 1681–1711.

28. Two tides this morning.

Feb. 3. This afternoon the gout swelled my hand again, and the night passed with great torment.

4. This night my hand did most grievously pain me.

Mar. 3. This afternoon I and my wife were both suddenly struck with a cold and hoarseness.

I felt the effects of this hoarseness, in the back part of my throat, for a long time after.

20. 2.30 p.m. An issue was made in my left arm.

April 16. My wife took Mr. Biggs his vomit, which wrought very well.

19. She took *Pulvis Sanctus*, in the afternoon she took cold. *N.B.* That both were too strong physic for her.

21. My wife fell very ill, and into great weakness.

26. I purged with my usual pills.

27. I took my usual sweat.

Toward the end of this month my wife began to mend, but did not fully recover of a fortnight after.

July 16. This morning I received a parcel of books from Jac. W. Im Hoff of Nurembergh, among which was his *Excellentium Familiarum in Gallia Genealogiæ*.

Aug. 31. Sir John Chardin,[1] came to South-Lambeth, to visit me with Mr. Bever.

Sept. 14. 10.40 a.m. I sat for a second picture to Mr. Ryley.[2]

Oct. 5. 11.7 a.m. The Earl Marshal's Court first sat in the Painted-Chamber, Westminster.

7. Dr. Plot came to me at my office, and told me, the Earl Marshal had chosen him Register of his Court.

[John Gadbury sent figures on nativities. MS. *Ashmole* 436.]

8. 10 a.m. I went first to the Earl Marshal's Court, and when his Lordship rose, he invited me to dine with him, which I did.

9. I took my usual sweat.

End of MS. Ashmole 1136.

---

[1] Sir JOHN CHARDIN, 1643–1713, travelling jeweller, knighted 1681 ; F.R.S. 1682.

[2] JOHN RYLEY, painter of the portraits of A. of 1683 and 1687, formerly in the Ashmolean Museum.

1688

Some of the events of the last five years
of Ashmole's life are indicated by letters
included in MS. *Rawlinson* D. 864.

For instance on *Oct.* 15. Dean Addison
and the chapter of Lichfield cathedral wrote
begging for a subscription £80 towards
finishing the ring of ten bells.

Oct. 15.   A. received the following letter
from Mr. Joshua Barnes of Cambridge, to
which he replied on the 23rd.

For the Worſhipful and Learned *Elias Aſh-*
mole, Eſq ; at his Houſe in *South-Lam-*
beth, near *London*.

Moſt worthy and learned Sir,

BEING informed by my Friend *Gad-*
bury, that there were ſeveral Paſſages
in my Hiſtory, which did ſome way re-
flect on your great Worth and Learning,
and alſo intimate me to be guilty of groſs
Rudeneſs and Heat.   I found it my Duty
to make this Recantation ; and ſo let you
know that whatever in that Kind may occurr,
I utterly repent and diſown ; and am both

heartily forry and afhamed, that any way I
fhould prove fo unhappily offenfive to fo
good and learned, fo induftrious and renowned a Gentleman, whofe Books I am not
worthy to bear after him. And, Sir, if it
will pleafe you to let me fee a Copy of the
Paffages, as you have collected them, (which
on Occafion I promife to return) with your
Confutations and Reafons annexed, I do
folemnly proteft that I will make a publick
Recantation, or otherwife as you fhall think
fit ; and alfo if ever King *Edward* fees
another Impreffion, I will alter thofe Paffages as far as Truth and Equity fhall
acquire, ftill protefting in *Verbo Sacerdotis*,
that I never had any but Honourable and
refpectful Thoughts of you and Sir *William
Dugdale*, (*Dii ! quanta nomina*) and what I
did, proceeded from a Defire of finding out
the Truth, however my Frailty might betray
me to an Error ; *Sir*, the Honour of a Line,
efpecially with an Intimation of your good
Will, will be highly acceptable to the real
Honourer of your Learning and Goodnefs.

Emanuel College, Camb.
 Oct. 15. 1688. *Jofhua Barnes*.

 My humble Duty to his Grace at *Lambeth*,
and pray, Sir, have me recommended to my

good Master Doctor *Goad* and Mr. *Gadbury*,
&c.

MS. *Ashmole* 1136 f. 133.

For my worthy Friend Mr. *Joshua Barnes*,
at *Emanuel-College* in *Cambridge*.[1]

SIR,

MY present weak Indisposition has took
me off from too much resenting
those Reflections you have made on me in
your Book,[2] and moulded in me more peace-
able Thoughts, than to be disturbed at what
you have done. Your Letter makes me
think there was no ill Meaning in what you
did, and perhaps nothing more than an
Inadvertent and overhasty Humour, which
the Civility of a Penny-Post Letter would
have cleared and prevented. I need not
trouble my self, nor you, with giving you an
Account of those Passages that concern me,
they are easily found out ; for they carry
my Name along with them. All I expect

---

[1] MS. *Ashmole* 1136.
[2] The *History of King Edward the IIId,* Fol. wherein
Mr. Barnes reflected on Mr. Ashmole's *Order of the Garter*
in a very gross manner.

from you is, that your Acknowledgments to others (as you have Occafion) be what you have now made to me, and (if ever an Opportunity be offered) to reprint your Hiftory, then to rectifie your Copy.

SIR,

I am
Your very Humble Servant,

E. Afhmole.

Octob. 23, 1688.

MS. *Ashmole* 1136 f. 136.

1689

1689 *Aug.* 12. "Mr. Ashmole, our common friend had collected all the ancient and modern coins of this kingdom, which were very rare, together with several medals of our British, Saxon and other kings, upon occasion of births, coronations, marriages, and other ceremonies. I know not whether they escaped the burning of his study at the Middle Temple." Evelyn in a *Letter* to Pepys.

1691

Ashmole's friends again tried to persuade him to stand for Lichfield,—the correspondence is preserved in MS. *Rawlinson* D. 864—but he was too near the end of his strength for such an enterprise; and in the spring of the next year he died.

1692

His will is at Somerset House.[1]

WILL OF ELIAS ASHMOLE
of the Middle Temple, London, ESQRE.,
dated : 6 September, 1686.

" I bequeath to the Chancellor, Masters
and Scholars of the University of Oxford all
my manuscript books and other manuscript
papers not yet sorted nor bound up books of
copper cuts and books ' lynned in colours '
and all my printed books in the two upper-
most turrets at my house in South Lambeth to
be preserved in the Museum Ashmoleanum
in presses, with locks and keys to be provided for them. Also I give to the said
Chancellor, Masters and Scholars the gold
chain and medal thereat depending bestowed
on me by the now King of Denmark and
the medal sent me by his Electoral Highness
of Brandenburgh, the gold medal of Charles
Prince Elector sent me from his son Charles
late Prince Elector and the George of gold
which Thomas, late Earl of Arundell and
Surrey wore in his journey to Vienna in
1636 and given me by Henry, late Duke of

[1] P.C.C. Fane, 97.

Norfolk, his grandson ; also the following pictures :—James I in his youth, Charles I, Dr. John Dee, Mr. Richard Napier, Dr. Nicholas Fiske, Mr. William Lilly the Astrologian, Mr. John Lowen the Comedian, Capt. Burgh and the old painted draught of Henry VIII's monument to be placed in the said Museum ; also the pamphlets, newsbooks, poems, books of controversy relating to religion, the late wars and these later times bound up stitched or loose which are in the Inward Closet within my lower study over the milkhouse in my said house at South Lambeth to be likewise placed in the Museum. Also the picture of Sir Francis Crane, Knt., sometime Chancellor of the Order of the Garter to the Alms Knights of his foundation within the Castle of Windsor to be placed in the building of his erection there.

Whereas I am possessed of a messuage in South Lambeth, Co. Surrey, wherein I now dwell, for the residue of a term of 500 years, the inheritance whereof conveyed to John Dugdale of Coventry, Esqre., and his heirs in trust for me and my heirs or such persons as I shall name in my will, I bequeath the said messuage to my wife Elizabeth and her heirs and I give her also my burgage house in Bird Street, Lichfield.

Whereas I lately purchased a messuage and lands in South Lambeth of John Plummer, gent., I give the same to my wife and her heirs for ever.

To my cousin Thomas Ashmole son of my uncle John Ashmole, £10.

To the children of my cousin, John Ashmole, eldest son of my said uncle, 5s. each.

To my cousin Sarah [left blank] and her son, my godson, William Tompson, £5 each.

To the children of my uncle, Ralph Ashmole, 5s. each.

To my cousin Samuel Storey, £10.

To my cousin George Smalridge, student at Christchurch, Oxford, all the works of Albertus Magnus containing 17 volumes, printed at Lyons in France, 1651.

Residuary legatee and executrix : my wife Elizabeth.

Signed :—E. Ashmole.

Witnesses :—Sa. Story, Tho. Smith, Willm. Clarke, Jo. Streets.

Codicil dated 11 December, 1689.

I desire my wife to give to my sister, Mrs. Dorothy Manwaring, £100.

Signed :—E. Ashmole.

Proved :—11 June, 1692, by Elizabeth Ashmole, the relict and executrix."

Mr. John Aubrey, F.R.S., in his *Survey of the County of Surry*, (reposited in the Ashmolean Museum) towards the beginning has these words—"And now I am come "as a Mourner to perform my laſt Office at the "Grave of my worthy Friend *Elias Ashmole*, "Eſq ; whoſe Body lieth buried in the *South* "Ile (of the Church of *South-Lambeth*) at the "*East* End, on the *North* Side of it, under a "black Marble, with this Inscription.

Hic jacet Inclytus Ille & Eruditissimus
ELIAS ASHMOLE Leichfeldensis Armiger,
inter alia in Republica Munera,
Tributi in Cerviſias Contra Rotulator,
Fæcialis autem Windſorienſis *titulo*
per annos plurimos dignatus,
Qui poſt duo connubia in Uxorem duxit tertiam
Elizabetham *GULIELMI DUGDALE*
Militis, Garteri, Principalis Regis Armorum
filiam ;
Mortem obiit 18 *Maii,* 1692. *anno ætatis* 76.
Sed durante Muſæo ASHMOLEANO, Oxon.
nunquam moriturus.

Near it, is an achievement set up for the same person, whereon is the coat of arms *of Ashmole*, viz. Quarterly sable and or, on the first quarter a fleur-de-lis of the second ; impaling *Dugdale*, viz. Argent, a cross moline gules, and a torteau ; with the motto —*Ex uno omnia.*

It should be noted that in accordance with his Will, Ashmole's manuscripts and a part of his library of printed books were not consigned to the Bodleian Library, but were appropriately housed in the Ashmolean Museum in a room specially fitted for their reception. They were thereby placed in the custody of the Keepers of the Natural History Museum of the University, an arrangement which had then such obvious advantages that several of Oxford's greatest benefactors followed Ashmole's example, and left their collections for preservation and use in his Building.

Over the door of the Library, was placed the following inscription, in letters of gold,

Libri Impreſſi & Manuſcripti e donis Clariſſ. Virorum D. Eliæ *Aſhmole &* Martini Liſter *Quibus non paucos addidit Vir induſtrius nec*

infime de Re Antiquariâ Promeritus D. Johannes Aubrey *de* Eaſton Peirce *apud* Wiltonienſes *Arm. & Soc. Reg. Socius.*

Anthony Wood, Borlase, and others left books to the same Library. But in the ill-conceived rearrangements that were carried out during the second half of the nineteenth century, collections became separated from the books about them, and important catalogues were divorced from historic collections, with the result that the latter were rendered useless and were eventually lost or destroyed as " of no scientific value."

1693–4

On *Feb.* 22, the remainder of Ashmole's Library was sold by auction at Roll's Auction House in Petty Canon Alley in St. Paul's Churchyard. It consisted of seventy-nine miscellaneous books in folio, fifty-one in quarto, and fifty-seven in octavo : 190 miscellaneous books in folio, 100 in quarto, and 305 in octavo. There were also 12 folio, 14 quarto and 4 octavo manuscripts. The catalogue, entitled *Bibliotheca Ashmoliana*, was drawn up by Edward Millington.

AN APPENDIX

Of Original Letters sent to, and from
Mr. Ashmole.

A Letter of Thanks (MS. *Ashmole* 1136
f. 104) *from the Corporation of Lichfeld,
upon the receipt of a Silver Bowl, Presented
to them by Mr. Ashmole.*

For the truly Honoured *Elias Ashmole*, Esq ;
at his Chamber in the *Middle Temple*,
over Serjeant *Maynard's* Chamber. In
his Absence, to be left with the Butler or
Porter of the *Middle-Temple, London.*

Honoured Sir,

UPON Thursday, being the 17th Day of
this Instant *January* (a Day ever to
be *Rubrical* amongst our City Remem-
brances) we received your *Tina Argentea,*
your munificent Silver Bowl, cloathed in its
Delivery, with all those Rich Circumstances
of Advantage, that could possibly either
enable the Gift to bespeak the Goodness

L

and Prudence of the Giver, or invite the
faireſt Acceptation in the Receiver. For if
we conſider the Perſon from whom : It is
the Gift of an *Elias*, a Herald, not only
Proclaiming, but actually Contributing good
Things to our City ; and that by the Hands
of a *Zacharias*, a faithful Meſſenger, who
with the Gift, did emphatically communicate
the Senſe and good Affection of the Giver.
And if we conſider the time it was Preſented ;
It was the Day of our *Epiphany* Seſſions of
the Peace for this City, where our Bailiffs,
High-Steward, Sheriff, Grand Jury, and the
reſt of the Body Politick of this Antient and
Loyal Corporation, together with other
Perſons of Quality, both of the Clergy and
Laity were convened together, and ſo became
preſent at this great Offering : As if ſome
propitious Stars ariſing in the Eaſt, had (at
this time) gone before our *Magus*, ſteering
its Course to this our City of *Lichfeld* (the
Sarepta of our *Elias*) and ſtood over the New-
Erected Pyramids of our Cathedral (where
as yet a Star appears) darting its benign
Influence upon this Poor and Loyal City,
inviting the *Magi* from afar, to offer ſome
Tribute to it. A City that hath nothing to
glory in, but its Antient and Modern Loyalty
to God and *Cæſar*, evidenced by her antient

Bearing in the City Efcotcheon (three
Knights martyred) as antient as the Days of
Dioclefian, and her Name fignifying a Field
of Blood then fpilt, to which may be well
added her Modern and unparallelled Loyalty to that Bleffed Saint (now in Heaven)
King *Charles* the Martyr ; Univerfally wit-
neffed by thofe honourable Marks, Eraces,
and Wounds of Loyalty, fhe yet bears upon
her Perfons, Temples, Streets, and Walls ;
(Trophies of Honour) fufficiently blazing to
the World the true Heraldry of her ancient
Arms ; nor have you only given us this
great *Cratera* (upon which you have wifely
impreft our City-Arms) to folace the beft of
the City, after their Time of Suffering, but
like one of thofe true *Magi*, that offered to
Chrift in his pooreft Condition, you have
largely offered to the Repair of his Church,
our ruined Cathedral, which, by the un-
wearied Labour, Prudence, Piety, and Charity of our good [1] Bifhop, a fecond *Cedda*,
and the Charity of your felf, and others
happily depofited in his Hands, is (almoft
to a Miracle) fo well and fo foon reftored
again. But you have likewife Annually and
liberally offered, relieved, and refrefhed

[1] Dr. Hacket.

Chrift in his Members, the Poor of our
City. And as if you intended pioufly to
ingrofs and cover all our Neceffities, under
that warm and nourifhing Mantle of *Elias*,
we have received Intimation of your Pro-
mifes of greater Good intended this great
City. Now, Sir, give us Leave to conclude
(having been already too tedious) by inform-
ing you that, according to your Defire,
(upon the firft Receipt of your *Poculum
Charitatis*, at the Sign of the *George* for
England) we filled it with Catholick Wine,
and devoted it a fober Health to our moft
gracious King, which (being of fo large a
Continent, paft the Hands of Thirty to
pledge ; nor did we forget your felf in the
next Place, being our great *Mæcænas* ; affur-
ing you that (God willing) we fhall take
Courfe that this great *Tina Argentea* fhall,
with our City-Mace, and other publick
Enfigns of Dignity and Authority, be care-
fully tranfmitted, by Indenture, from Bailiffs
to Bailiffs, in a continual Succeffion, fo long
as this ancient and loyal Corporation through
the Favour of Princes (which we hope, we
fhall never forfeit) fhall have a Charter to
give it Life and Being. For which End
your many other multiplied Favours to this
poor City, We, the prefent Bailiffs of this

City, do, in the Name (and by the Defire) of our whole Company, return you moſt hearty Thanks, ſubſcribing our ſelves what we truly are,

SIR,

Your obliged faithful Friends,

Lichfeld, 26.   To serve you,
Jan. 1666.

John Barnes,
Hen. Baker.

A Preface to the Catalogue of Archbiſhop Laud's Medals, drawn up by Mr. Aſhmole, and preſerved in the publick Library at Oxford, and referred to in page 78 of this Work.

Lectori Benevolo, εὖ πράττειν καὶ εὐδαιμονεῖν.

CUM Oxoniam (Britannici lumen orbis primarium, grandeque decus) commentandi gratiâ annos aliquot ante me contuliſſem, Collegio Reginenſi Præpoſiti (tunc temporis autem in inclytâ hac Univerſitate, Proto-Bibliothecarii Bodleiani) Doctoris Barlow poſtulatio, imo & expoſtulatio, me non mediocriter afficere [sic : add potuerunt ?]

Querebatur enim eximiæ doctrinæ Vir,

inter Academicos, (temporibus difficillimis illis quidem, & tyrannide *Cromwelliana* invalefcente, duriffimis) paucos tum super-effe (plurimis, artis & naturæ dotibus fufpiciendis, Oftracifmo etiamnum pulfis, aut (nec vanus timor) propediem pellendis) qui ad rei Antiquariæ ftudium & veterum Numifmatum cognitionem, quibus tamen affatim illic abundent Archiva, (paupertate & nova tyrannide preffi) adjeciffent animum. Supra laudati *Doctoris*, inquam, rogatu, conquestuque, hoc ultro mihimet (ut brevem illorum defcriptionem exhiberem) penfum impofui : tum ad novitios & in rei Nummariæ fcientiâ parum exercitatos, melius informandos, tum ad eorum Genium excitandum, qui ad tantum, tam proficuum, tam dignum, tam honorificum, tam denique neceffarium erudito viro ftudium afpirare niterentur.

Hoc igitur fic mihi propofitum fponteque fufceptum (arduum illud quidem, & laboriosæ plenum opus aleæ penfum) lætus aggredior, indies factione *Cromwelliana*, non fine damno publico, ingravefcente, & paulo poft Britanniæ παλιγγενεσίαν & facræ Regiæ Majeftatis (aufpicatò & quafi poftliminio) reditum, σὺν Θεῶ ad finem perduxi. Sed cum hujus exfcriptum, manu propria cuperem exarare, ut ingenuè fatear, mihi fuit ἀδύνατον

ante hunc diem illud abfolvere, cum nego-
tiorum (quæ me continuò circumvallat)
turba, modicum mihi fubinde fpatium, ad
aliquid per intervalla et quafi furtim non-
nunquam ex eo tranfcribendum permiferit.
Verum antequam huic Operi confiderando
te Lector accingas, de nonnullis, & ad promp-
tiorem ejus intelligentiam, & ad faciliorem
ejufdem ufum, te monitum cupio.

Atque ut aggrediar, totum opus de anti-
quis Numifmatis quibus *Oxoniæ* ditefcunt
Archiva, in tria dividitur Volumina. Pri-
mum eft *Confularium Nummorum, aliquotque
Illuftrium Romæ Familiarum*, reliqua duo
Imperatoria Numifmata continent.

Huc accedit, quòd Monetam Confulum
alphabetico locarim ordine potius, quam
illam in annorum Confulatus cujufque feriem
redigerim : multi etenim Confulares
Nummi, nequaquam ab iis, quibus affimi-
lantur, excufi funt. Sed ab illis Trium-
viris Monetalibus *Augufti* regno, qui vellent
ifta ratione, vel quod forfan ab ipfis ducerent
originem, ut præclaras illorum actiones
aliquot exciperet ac tueretur æternitas.
Quod autem attinet ad *Imperiales* Nummos
(qui hic incipiunt à *Julio Cæfare*, atque cum
Heraclio definunt) hi ad eos perfectè refer-
untur annos, in quibus conflati, procufique

fuere ; cum relatione tamen ad tempus vel
præcedens, vel fubfequens Incarnationem
Chrifti Salvatoris noftri, quod characteribus
iftis expreffi, A. C. hoc eft, ante Incarnationem *Chrifti*, & I. C. id eft, ab Incarna-
tione *Chrifti*. Qui characteres notantur in
capite cujuflibet paginæ, paucis exceptis, qui
fufficiens ad hoc, ut ad manifeftam fui temporis cognitionem deducere me queant,
lumen defiderare videntur. Atque iftos
quidem fub *Imperatoris* cujufque regni finem,
anno ante eofdem in margine nullo defignato,
collocare, quam eofdem cæteros inter in-
trudere certâ fine ratione, fatius elegi.
Idemque circa *Imperatrices* omnes, eandem-
que ob rationem, a me præftitum eft.

Præterea, ut ex quo genere metalli quodli-
bet ex dictis Numifmatis cufum eft, conftare
poffit ; metalla per has fequentes diftinxi
notas AV. enim denotat *aurum*, AR. indicat
argentum, Æ denique fignificat *Æs*.

Porro cum Ænei Nummi diverfæ magnitudinis exiftant ; ad triplicem præfertim
(qua dignofcantur) juxta numericas figuras
(1.) (2.) & (3.) characteribus illorum præfixas
(exceptis parvulis valdeque minutis aliquot,
qui peculiariter pro talibus exhibentur) ad
triplicem, inquam, præcipue magnitudinem,
revocari poffunt.

Adde superioribus, quod ubi quempiam argenteum Nummum, formam habentem secundæ magnitudinis æreorum invenio, quod ut duxtaxat ab ordinario distinguatur Denario, figuram illi (2.) soleam adjungere.

Hanc, hoc gemino cum voto, præfatiuncu-lam claudere mihi est animus, D. O. M. enixè deprecatus, tum ut generoforum hâc in parte Benefactorum numerum adaugeat : tum ut eos qui prisca Numismata celeberri-mum hoc in Ærarium conferunt, novis, quibus suam sublevent inopiam, Numis-matis, nunquam egere patiatur.

Pene omiseram quemlibet post annum, hic a me de industria relictum esse spatium, ut qui de novo dictum ad Thesaurum, antiqui ferentur Nummi, ad hunc quoque Catalogum, pari (quo superiores) modo, referri valeant.

E. ASHMOLE.

Scriptum   in   meo
   Medii   Templi
   Musæo,   decimo
   Calendas   Junias,
   Anno   Juliano   1666.

A Letter from Doctor Barlow *to* Ashmole, *on his Present of his Books, describing Archbishop* Laud's *Cabinet of Medals.*

For my Honoured Friend *Elias Ashmole*, Efq, at his Chamber in the *Middle Temple*, thefe ; *London.*

My dear Friend,

IT is a good while fince I received your excellent Prefent to our Univerfity Library, and, 'ere this, told you fo ; and returned our many and hearty Thanks, had I not been fuddenly and unexpectedly called away to *Worcefter*, whence I am now returned. At the Vifitation of *Bodlyes* Library (when the Vice-Chancellor and all the Curators were met) I prefented your Books to the Vice-Chancellor, and the reft, in your Name, as a Teftimony of your Kindnefs and Love to Learning and our Univerfity ; as alfo of your Ability to enrich *Bodlyes* Library with your own Works : Any Man who has a Mind to it, and Money, may give us good Books of other Mens making, but very few of their own ; *pauci quos æquus amavit Jupiter.* Some more generous and ingenuous Souls, a *Selden*, a *Dugdale*, or an *Afhmole* may do this, none else. The Vice-Chancellor and the Curators were exceeding well-satisfied with, and very thankful for your great Charity and Munificence to the Publick. Care is taken, that your Name and Gift be recorded in our Register, to your deserved Honour, and the Incouragement of others ; by your good Example, if not to an Equal, yet to a like Liberality. And sure I am, it will be an Honour to you, and a Comfort to your Friends, when they shall find in our Register, that you have been so great a Benefactor to *Bodlyes* Library. My Love and Respects to your self and my honest Friend Mr. *Dugdale.* God Almighty bless you both, And,

> SIR,
>
> *Your affectionate Friend,*
> Thomas Barlow.

Queen's College, Oxon.   *Decemb.* 28, 1668.

Mrs. Tradescant's Submission to Elias Ashmole, Esq.

Bee it known unto all persons that I, Hester Tradescant, of S. Lamb., in the County of Surrey, widdow, doe acknowledge and confess, in the presence of Mr. Justice Dawling and other the witnesses hereunder subscribed, that I have very much wronged Elias Ashmole, Esquire, by several fals, scandalous, and defamatory speeches, re-

ports, and otherwise, tending to the diminu-
tion and blemishing of his reputation and
good name, more especially in these particu-
lars following :

First, I have reported to severall persons
that the said Elias Ashmole had made a dore
out of his garden into my orchard, by which
he might come into my house as soone as
the breath was out of my body, and take
away my goods ; whereas in truth there was
not, nor yet is, any such dore made by him.

Secondly, that he had taken away 250
foote of my ground, when he built his garden wall ; whereas his said wall was set in
the place where an old pale stood immediately before he built his wall, and was lyned
out in the presence of my cosen Blake the
plummer, whome my landlord Mr. Bartholomew had impowered on his behalf so to doe.

Thirdly, I have reported to severall persons, as well strangers as others of my acquaintance, that the said Mr. Ashmole had
forced me to deliver up to him my Closet
of Rarities, and that if I had not done [so]
he would have cut my throat ; and, in the
presence of diverse neighbours, I falsely
charged the said Mr. Ashmole that he had
robd me of my Closet of Rarities, and
cheated me of my Estate ; whereas, in truth,

I prest him to receive the said Rarities ;
and when he intreated me to keepe them,
and not only used many arguments to persuade me to it, but set on other of my friends
and neighbours to persuade me likewise, I
would not hearken to their advice, but forced
him to take them away, threatning, that if
he did not, I would throw them into the
streete, and he having at last consented to
receive them, I voluntarily helped to remove
some of them myselfe.

Fourthly, I reported that I had made him
promise me to bestow the said Rarities on
the University of Oxford, and that I would
force him to send them thither : whereas I
never moved the said Mr. Ashmole to any
such thing, when I delivered them to him,
or at any time since.

Fifthly, that I caused a great heape of
earth and rubbish to be laid against his
garden wall, so high, that on the sixt day
of August last in the night by the helpe
thereof, it is strongly presumed that thieves
got over the same, and robd the said Mr.
Ashmole of 32 cocks and hens ; and notwithstanding he admonished me to take it
away, I told him it should be there in spight
of his teeth ; and so it continued untaken
away above six weeks after he was so robbed,

whereby he lay in continual fear of having his house broken open every night.

All which, and many other like false and scandalous reports and words, as I have unadvisedly and rashly spoken against him, without any provocation of his in words or deedes, so am I really and heartily sorry that I have so greatly wronged him therein ; and have, in the presence of the said Mr. Justice Dawling and the subscribed wit nesses, acknowledged the said wronge and injuries so done unto the said Mr. Ashmole, and asked him publique forgiveness for the same ; and doe hereby voluntarily and freely promise the said Mr. Ashmole that no manner of rubish or earth shall be layd against his said garden wall ; and that henceforth I will not say or doe anything against him or his wife, that may tend to the damage, reproach, or disreputation of them, or either of them. In witness where-of, I have hereunto set my hand, the first day September, 1676.

ESTER TREDUSCANT.

Subscribed in the presence of Jo. Dau-linge, Tho. Bedford, Rich. Kendall, Tho: de Critz, Tho. Murrey, Garrud Sraugh, K. King, Geo. Worge.

For *Elias Ashmole*, Esq ; at his House in
Lambeth.

SIR,

THE Bearer hereof will need no Recommendation from me, when you shall
understand, that it is Doctor *Plott*, the
learned Author, of the natural History of
Oxfordshire. It is upon the Reputation of
your own Worth, as well as your magnificent
Gift intended to the University, that he has
the Ambition to be better known to you :
They are (I hear) designing to create a
Philosophical Lecture upon Natural Things,
and their Inclination to pitch upon this
knowing Gentleman for that Purpose (whose
Talent and Merits are so eminent) I am sure,
cannot miss of your concurrent Suffrage :
I am only sorry, that the Affair, which carries
me this Morning out of Town, deprives me
of so desired an Opportunity of kissing your
Hand at *Lambeth*, who am, for many great
Obligations.

SIR,

Your most Humble
And Obedient Servant,
J. EVELYN.

Whitehall, 7 Dec. 1677.
MS. *Ashmole* 1136 f. 114.

A Copy of a Letter from the Chapter of the Church of Lichfeld *to Mr.* Afhmole, *communicated from the* Regifters *of that Cathedral.*

Honoured Sir,

WHATEVER Intereft this City and Church have in your Birth and Education, hath already redounded, in fo much Honour thereby, and in your continual Bounty, to both : That we have not the Confidence to back with that Topick, this our Petition for your free Gift, towards finifhing the Ring of Ten Bells, inftead of our former Six bad and ufelefs ones. Nor, in Truth, have we any other Arguments, but your Charity and our Neceffity ; of the former, you have given us good Proof, as we acknowledge with all Thankfulnefs. And of the latter, we have too much, through the Misfortunes of the Work. The Deceitfulnefs of the Ground firft making our honeft Bell-Founder lofe his cafting the Four biggeft, to the Damage of £30 and now his Error in overfizing the Eight Bells, he hath caft, fo far that they have fwallowed up all the Metal for the Ten ; and that requires £80 more to be added to our poor Fund for the two other Bells, proportionable to that

Bignefs. But yet an Error fo much on the better Hand, that would make extreamly for the Advantage and Glory of the Cathedral (the Bignefs of fuch a Ring far more befitting the Place ; and thefe Eight being judged fo very good, that all are loth to have them broken, and caft into lefs) if poffibly that additional Sum could be raifed. To this purpofe Efq ; *Diot*, Mr. *Walmifley*, the Sub-Chantor, and other Vicars, and Ringers are moft induftrioufly undertaking a new Collection, and We and feveral others are willing a-new to contribute, and if you will pleafe to put to the helping Hand of your Piety and Munificence ; you will add fignally to thofe Inftances thereof already in our publick Catalogue of Benefactors, and will highly oblige both thofe zealous Under-takers, and efpecially,

   SIR,
    Your thankful humble Servants,
      Lanc. Addison,
      Hen. Greswold,
Lichfeld,   Tho. Browne,
 Oct. 15. Jo. Hutchinson.
 1688.   Chris. Comyn.

M

TRADESCANT'S HOROSCOPE AS CAST BY ASHMOLE,
MAY, 1652.

From Early Science in Oxford, vol. iii.

INDEX